SMALL OFFICES
PETITS BUREAUX
KLEINE BÜROS

SMALL OFFICES
PETITS BUREAUX
KLEINE BÜROS

EVErGrEEn

EVERGREEN is an imprint of

Taschen GmbH

© 2005 TASCHEN GmbH

Hohenzollernring 53, D-50672 Köln

www.taschen.com

Editorial project Projet éditorial Redaktionelle Umsetzung:

© 2005 Loft Publications

www.loftpublications.com

Editor Editrice Redakteur:
Simone Schleifer

French translation Traduction française Französische Übersetzung:
Marion Westerhoff

German translation Traduction alemande Deutsche Übersetzung:
Grusche Rosenkranz

English proof reading Relecture anglaise Korrektur lesen:
Matthew Clarke

Art director Direction artistique Art Direktor:
Mireia Casanovas Soley

Graphic design and layout Mise en page et maquette Graphische Gestaltung und Layout:
Diego González

Printed by Imprimé en Gedruckt durch:
Anman Gràfiques del Vallès, Spain

ISBN: 3-8228-4180-3

The design strategies for offices are as varied as the circumstances applying to each space. The incessant demand for workspace, especially in the big cities, has increased speculation and forced companies to make do with the small amount of space available to them. The search for an efficient reduction of office space has led to technological advances, new communications networks, and unusual working arrangements. The combination of the distinctive characteristics of contemporary design and lack of space has given rise to a phenomenon of great interest to both designers and companies forced to adapt to a confined workspace: the small office. Businesses express their own, unique identity by highlighting their corporate image. Different strategies are used in each office space to impart that identity, so design projects become laboratories of ideas for architects and designers. The limitations on the availability of space force both companies and designers to give priority to an office's functions in the design process.

Projects that confront a need to scale down generally share common features. With respect to furnishings, for example, internal partitions are highly important. New materials and light structures have made inflexible cubicles a relic of the past. Projects for small offices simplify the division of space as much as possible by ensuring that they are as compact as possible while providing the degree of privacy required in each case. Traditional materials such as glass and wood are now complemented by more recent arrivals, such as fiberglass and metallic mesh.

In some cases, all the furniture used for working can be easily stored away so that the office space can be put to other uses when necessary. For example, shelves can take on double functions in confined areas and also serve as internal dividers, line the walls, or be used as movable modules.

The shape, size, and placement of desks, tables, and counters are entirely determined by the type of work to be performed. Some of these work surfaces can function as conference tables while others can be moved to create combinations with other elements or be stored away.

This book examines the challenges posed by 26 design projects for small offices and examines the solutions reached by various world-famous designers and architects by drawing on their ingenuity and creativity.

Le design d'espace de bureaux varie en fonction des conditions spatiales données. La recherche croissante d'espace pour installer des bureaux, surtout dans les grandes villes, n'a fait qu'accroître la spéculation, forçant les compagnies à se contenter du moindre espace disponible. La réduction efficace de l'espace bureau est incontournable mais réalisable grâce aux progrès technologiques, aux nouveaux réseaux de communication et à de nouvelles méthodes de travail originales. L'alliance entre la diversité du design contemporain et le manque d'espace a engendré un phénomène particulièrement intéressant tant pour les designers que pour les sociétés, tous soumis à la même contrainte spatiale : les petits espaces de bureaux. Les entreprises expriment le caractère unique de leur identité en exaltant leur image de marque. A chaque espace de bureaux correspond une stratégie différente pour mettre en valeur cette identité. Les projets de design deviennent de véritables laboratoires d'idées pour architectes et designers. Les limitations de l'espace disponible forcent à la fois les compagnies et les designers à laisser la priorité à l'aspect fonctionnel du bureau dans la conception de l'espace.

Devant cette minimalisation forcée de l'espace, les projets partagent les mêmes idées. Au chapitre des meubles, par exemple, les cloisons revêtent une grande importance. Grâce aux nouveaux matériaux et aux structures légères, les cubes rigides sont devenus des reliques du passé. Les projets de petits bureaux simplifient la division de l'espace autant que faire se peut, en le rendant le plus compact possible, tout en gardant le degré d'intimité nécessaire. Aux matériaux classiques, tels que le verre et le bois, s'ajoutent des matières nouvelles, à l'instar de la fibre de verre et des filets et mailles métalliques.

Le cas échéant, tous les meubles utilisés dans le cadre du travail, au stockage facile, permettent un usage polyvalent des bureaux. Dans les petits espaces, les étagères, par exemple, peuvent avoir, tour à tour, plusieurs fonctions : cloisons intérieures, habillage de parois ou modules mobiles. Forme, taille et emplacement des bureaux, tables et comptoirs, dépendent entièrement du type de travail à accomplir.

Certaines de ces surfaces de travail font office de tables de conférences, d'autres, modulables, sont combinées à certains éléments ou tout simplement mises de côté.

Cet ouvrage présente les défis posés par 26 projets de design de petits espaces de bureaux et examine les solutions proposées par de prestigieux designers et architectes mondialement connus, fruit de leur ingéniosité et créativité artistique.

Die Designstrategien für Büros sind so unterschiedlich wie die Gegebenheiten der einzelnen Standorte. Der nicht nachlassende Bedarf an Büroräumen führt vor allem in den großen Städten zu immer mehr Spekulation und zwingt Unternehmen dazu, den ihnen zur Verfügung stehenden Platz optimal auszunutzen. Die Suche nach einer effektiven Verringerung des Platzbedarfs von Büros hat zu technologischen Neuerungen, neuen Kommunikationsnetzen und originellen Arbeitsumgebungen geführt. Die Kombination aus den besonderen Merkmalen des zeitgenössischen Designs und begrenztem Raum hat zu einer Entwicklung geführt, die sowohl Designer als auch Unternehmen dazu zwingt, sich an begrenzte Arbeitsplätze anzupassen. Das Kleinbüro wurde geboren. Unternehmen drücken ihre Identität aus, indem sie ihr besonderes Image hervorheben. Für jeden Bürobereich werden andere Strategien verwendet, um dieser Identität Rechnung zu tragen, so dass diese Projekte zu wahren Ideenschmieden für Architekten und Designer werden. Die durch den beschränkten Platz auferlegten Einschränkungen zwingen Unternehmen und Designer dazu, funktionalen Aspekten den Vorrang zu geben.

Diese Projekte haben in der Regel einige Gemeinsamkeiten. So sind beispielsweise, was die Einrichtung angeht, interne Abtrennungen besonders wichtig. Neue Materialien und leichte Strukturen haben dafür gesorgt, dass die starren Büroboxen der Vergangenheit angehören. Bei der Planung kleiner Büros wird die Raumteilung so weit wie möglich vereinfacht, indem die Büros so kompakt wie möglich ausgelegt werden und gleichzeitig einen hohen Grad an Privatsphäre bieten. Traditionelle Materialien wie Glas und Holz werden mit neuen Stoffen wie Glasfaser und Metallnetz kombiniert.

In manchen dieser Kleinbüros können die Arbeitsmöbel einfach beiseite geräumt und versteckt werden, so dass Platz für andere Verwendungszwecke entsteht. Regale dienen oft gleichzeitig auch als Raumteiler oder zum Abgrenzen oder werden als bewegliche Module benutzt.

Form, Gestalt, Größe und Platzierung von Schreibtischen, Abstelltischen und Bürotresen hängen ganz von der Art der Aktivität ab, für die der Raum dient. Einige der Arbeitsoberflächen können auch als Konferenztische genutzt werden, während andere verschoben werden können, um mit anderen Einrichtungselementen kombiniert oder versteckt zu werden.

Diese Buch zeigt anhand von 26 Kleinbüros die an die Designer gestellten Herausforderungen und untersucht die von diesen dafür gefundenen Lösungen, die sich allesamt durch Einfallsreichtum und Kreativität auszeichnen.

SMALL OFFICES
PETITS BUREAUX
KLEINE BÜROS

☐ Fast Forward

Propeller Z

An office that embodies a work of art could be the defining concept for this hybrid system, which offers the opportunity to sit down, recline, work at a computer, or store and display information. A horizontal platform from which parts have been removed, the system forms a kind of sinuous labyrinth that can accommodate each artist's needs. Its shape and dimensions can be adapted to spaces of varying proportions and requirements, thereby dramatically transforming the space it occupies. This single element is the solution to all matters of function, image, and flexibility. Individual parts can become independent modules, usable elsewhere as reception desks or conference tables, creating a universal image that can be adapted to any property. Moreover, this idea also works in small spaces, as there is no dividing element to break them up. The platform works like a huge, thick carpet engulfing a space and organizing its activities.

Un bureau, aux allures d'œuvre d'art, est une bonne description de ce système hybride offrant la possibilité de s'asseoir, s'incliner, travailler à l'ordinateur et enregistrer ou chercher des informations. Plate-forme horizontale, dépourvue de tout élément, le système forme une sorte de labyrinthe sinueux, modulable au gré des besoins de l'artiste. Sa forme et ses dimensions adaptables à un éventail de formes et d'exigences diverses, peut transformer complètement l'espace qu'il occupe. Cet élément unique résout toutes les questions de fonction, d'image et de flexibilité. Des parties indépendantes, transformées en modules, sont utilisables partout, à l'instar d'un bureau de réception ou de tables de conférences, créant un modèle universel adaptable en tous lieux. De plus, l'absence de cloisons permet aussi d'appliquer cette idée à des espaces réduits. La plate-forme se présente comme un énorme tapis épais, s'engouffrant dans l'espace et déployant ses activités.

Ein Büro, das einem Kunstwerk gleicht, könnte diesem hybriden System als Konzept zugrunde liegen. Eine horizontale Plattform, von der einzelne Teile entfernt wurden, bildet ein System mit einer Art Labyrinth. Seine Form und die Abmessungen können an verschiedene Proportionen und Anforderungen in Bezug auf Raum und Nutzen angepasst werden und beeinflussen so dominant den umgebenden Raum. Dieses Einzelelement bietet eine Lösung für alle Angelegenheiten im Hinblick auf Funktion, Image und Flexibilität. Einzelne Teile können als unabhängige Module auch anderswo als Empfangs- oder Konferenztisch dienen. So schafft man ein universelles Image, das an jeden beliebigen Raum angepasst werden kann. Diese Idee ist auch in kleinen Räumen einsetzbar, da keine Trennelemente erforderlich sind. Die Plattform dient als großer, dicker Teppich, auf dem die einzelnen Aktivitäten ausgeführt werden können.

The modules are independent and serve as individual workstations, but retain the same formal and functional language.

Les modules sont indépendants et servent d'unités de travail individuelles tout en gardant le même langage formel et fonctionnel.

Die Module sind unabhängig und dienen als individuelle Arbeitsplätze während. Form und funktionales Design gleich bleiben.

...e piece is more than just a work surface for artists, for it can also function as a platform for displays and customer service.

...'œuvre est plus qu'un plan de travail pour artistes, car il fait aussi office de plate-forme d'exposition ou de service clientèle.

...as Element dient nicht nur als Arbeitsfläche für Künstler, es kann gleichzeitig als Plattform für Ausstellungen und Kundenbetreuung dienen.

□ BBH

Klein Dytham Architecture

Located in a typical Tokyo office building, the main condition of this project was to create a space for a growing company that would move to larger premises in the near future. Thus, the project had to fit the space out with components that could be easily dismantled when they had to be moved. The walls and ceiling were not touched, since they would have to be left in their original state when the space was vacated. The refurbishment brought out the best in the available space, using a linear layout to create a feeling of roominess. The U-shaped meeting room reflects concepts derived from traditional Japanese culture and seems to float above the bright red floor. Silver curtains afford privacy when necessary and darkness for viewing videos or slides. Lacquered surfaces, the U shape repeated in the furniture in the reception area, and a combination of warm and fluorescent lighting have crafted a sparkling, luminous space.

Situé dans un immeuble de bureaux typique de Tokyo, ce projet a pour tâche de créer un espace adaptable à une compagnie en plein essor, bientôt amenée à changer de locaux. Il est donc impératif d'y intégrer des éléments facilement démontables en cas de déménagement. Les murs et plafonds ont été laissés intacts, pour garder leur état d'origine au moment du transfert. Pour optimiser l'espace disponible, la rénovation a eu recours à une conception créant une sensation d'amplitude. La salle de réunion en forme de U, est le reflet de concepts issus de la culture japonaise et semble flotter au-dessus du sol rouge vif. Des rideaux argentés favorisent l'intimité et créent l'obscurité requise pour visionner vidéos ou diapositives. Les surface laquées, la forme en U qui se retrouve dans le mobilier de la zone de réception et un mélange d'éclairage chaleureux et fluorescent parachèvent la signature de cet espace superbe et lumineux.

Das Büro von BBH wurde in einem typischen Bürogebäude Tokios untergebracht. Ziel der Projektgestaltung war es, einem wachsenden Unternehmen Raum zu schaffen, das schon bald in größere Räume umziehen würde. Es ging also hauptsächlich darum, den Raum mit Komponenten zu füllen, die bei einem Umzug leicht wieder abgebaut werden könnten. Wände und Decken blieben unangetastet. Mit einem linearen Layout wurde ein Gefühl von Weite geschaffen. Der in U-Form gehaltene Konferenzraum reflektiert Konzepte aus der traditionellen Kultur Japans und scheint förmlich über dem tiefroten Boden zu schweben. Silberne Vorhänge bieten die erforderliche Privatsphäre und Dunkelheit, um Videos oder Dias anzuschauen. Gelackte Oberflächen, die U-Form, die sich auch in den Möbeln im Empfangsbereich widerspiegelt, und ein Zusammenspiel von warmen, fluoreszierenden Leuchten sorgen für einen Energie geladenen, hellen Raum.

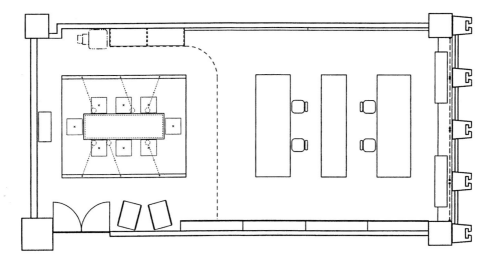

Plan Plan Grundriss

The low, black-lacquered conference table and blue cushions accentuate the project's references to traditional Japanese culture.

La table de conférence, basse et laquée de noir, conjuguée aux coussins bleus, souligne les références faites aux traditions de la culture japonaise.

Der niedrige, schwarze Konferenztisch und die blauen Kissen sind eine Referenz an die traditionelle japanische Kultur.

The furnishings—including, in this case, the meeting room itself—project the image of a youthful, innovative company.

L'agencement -y compris la salle de réunion- projette l'image d'une compagnie jeune et innovatrice.

Einrichtung und Konferenzraum an sich geben dem Projekt ein jugendliches, innovatives Image, das dem des Unternehmens entspricht.

☐ Glen Irani

Glen Irani Architects

The main requirement of the client, an architect, was to combine his family home with his workplace and to accommodate a number of activities, such as small social or professional receptions, after-hours reading, and weekend leisure activities in the garden. To make the best use of the available space and maximize flexibility, the architect designed four wheeled workstations that could be easily moved along a rail to be stored away to the rear. The electrical equipment and the lighting fixtures are independent of the desks, to further facilitate their movement. The work modules consist of a curved piece of sheet metal that functions as a work surface and side support and is connected to the long rail. The longitudinal layout forced on the space meant that these were placed one behind the other, in alignment with the swimming pool. A dramatic effect was created by placing the office at a level slightly below the swimming pool and raising its ceiling.

La requête principale du client, architecte, était de réunir son domicile et son bureau et d'y héberger certaines activités : petites réceptions sociales ou professionnelles, lectures après le travail, pratique de loisirs dans le jardin. Pour tirer le meilleur parti de l'espace disponible et en optimaliser la flexibilité, l'architecte a dessiné quatre modules de travail sur roues, pouvant être déplacés le long d'un rail et rangés à l'arrière. Pour plus de mobilité, le système électrique et l'éclairage sont indépendants du bureau. Ces modules sont constitués d'une feuille de métal incurvée comme plan de travail et support latéral, connectée au rail. Dû à la conception longitudinale imposée à l'espace, ces unités sont placées l'une derrière l'autre et parallèles à la piscine. L'architecte a réussi un superbe effet de mise en scène, en plaçant le bureau légèrement en contrebas de la piscine et en surélevant le plafond.

Der Kunde, selbst Architekt, wollte in diesem Haus Familie und Büro unter einem Dach vereinen und gleichzeitig eine Reihe anderer Aktivitäten ermöglichen, wie z.B. Familienfeste, Lesungen oder Freizeitaktivitäten am Wochenende im Garten. Um den verfügbaren Raum so gut wie möglich zu nutzen und gleichzeitig flexibel zu bleiben, haben die Architekten vier mit Rädern versehene Arbeitsplätze entwickelt, die über eine Schiene im hinteren Bereich gelagert werden können. Die Verkabelung und Beleuchtung wurden unabhängig von den Schreibtischen angebracht. Die Arbeitsmodule bestehen aus einem gebogenen Stück Blech, das als Arbeitsplatte und seitliche Verstärkung dient und an der langen Schiene angebracht ist. Der längliche Grundriss des Raumes bedingt die Installation der Arbeitsplätze hintereinander und in Ausrichtung zum Pool. Einen dramatischen Effekt erzielt die Platzierung des Büros ein kleines Stück unterhalb des Pools mit gleichzeitiger Erhöhung der Decke.

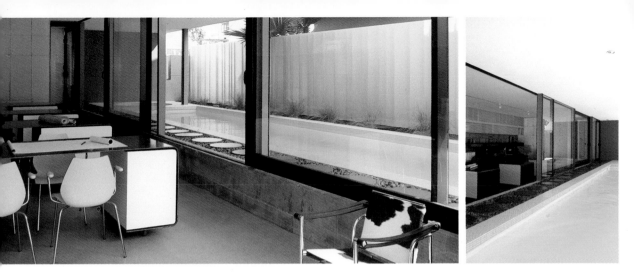

]
lacing the office at a level slightly below the swimming pool creates a dramatic effect and allows for a higher ceiling in the office.

e bureau placé légèrement en contrebas de la piscine, est une mise en scène grandiose qui permet une hauteur de plafond plus importante.

Das Büro liegt etwas tiefer der Pool, was einen atemberaubenden Effekt erzeugt und somit höhere Decken im Büro ermöglicht.

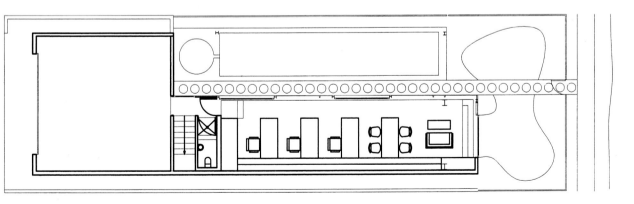

Plan Plan Grundriss

ar accommodates a small reading area that communicates with the community garden.

in lecture se trouve à côté du jardin, à l'arrière du bâtiment.

kseitigen Garten gleich neben dem Gebäude befindet sich eine Leseecke.

☐ Bates Smart

Bates Smart Pty Ltd.

The firm Bates Smart, which has offered complete architectural services since 1852, designed their own headquarters in Melbourne. The design, which clearly expresses the spirit of this architectural studio, consists of a series of pavilions that are inserted into the white volumes which form the space. The objectives throughout are homogeneity and a sense of unity; as a result, white was chosen as the dominant color, and the space was handled in terms of its overall context. Although each of the various zones occupied by the company's different departments were designed individually and clearly defined, they all form part of a unified whole. They are bright, open, functional, and easily defined work spaces that are perceived as luminous and ordered interiors, providing the perfect framework for the activities carried out within them. Although the materials and colors are limited in range, the furniture design is more outgoing and richer in nuances.

La société Bates Smart, bureau d'architecture depuis 1852, a conçu son propre siège à Melbourne. Le design, parfaite expression de l'esprit de ce studio d'architecture, prévoit une série de pavillons insérés dans un espace de volumes blancs. Les principes de base, l'homogénéité et le sens de l'unité ont déterminé le choix du blanc comme couleur dominante et l'espace est traité dans son contexte global. Même si les diverses zones occupées par les différents services de la compagnie sont conçues individuellement et clairement définies, elles sont toutes parties intégrante d'une unité. Ce sont des espaces de bureau larges, ouverts, fonctionnels et facilement définissables, aux intérieurs lumineux et bien agencés, cadre parfait pour les activités qu'ils abritent. Si l'éventail des matériaux et des couleurs est limité, le design du mobilier se décline dans une palette de teintes plus riches et vives.

Das Unternehmen Bates Smart, das bereits seit 1852 als Architekturbüro eingetragen ist, hat seine eigene Hauptgeschäftsstelle in Melbourne entworfen. Der Entwurf besteht aus einer Reihe von Pavillons, die in große, weiße Räume eingebunden sind. Vorrangiges Ziel war die Homogenität und ein Gefühl von Vereinigung. Daher wurde die Farbe Weiß auch als vorherrschende Farbe gewählt und der Raum in Bezug auf seinen Gesamtkontext behandelt. Obwohl jeder der Bereiche, die von den einzelnen Abteilungen des Unternehmens besetzt werden, unabhängig voneinander und eindeutig definiert wurde, bilden sie doch ein vereintes Ganzes. So entstanden hier helle, offene, funktionelle und einfach zu definierende Arbeitsbereiche, die sowohl leuchtende als auch geordnete Innenräume aufweisen und so das perfekte Rahmenwerk für die darin ausgeführten Arbeiten bieten. Obwohl Materialien und Farben begrenzt wurden, fallen die Möbel aus dem Rahmen und warten mit pfiffigen Details auf.

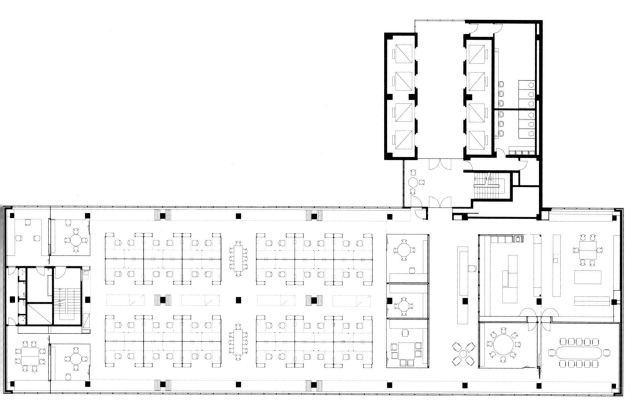

Plan Plan Grundriss

The materials and color range are deliberately limited. In contrast, the choice of furniture, with respect to models, colors and textures, is more generous and richer in nuances.

L'éventail de matériaux et de couleurs est délibérément limité. Il contraste avec la richesse et l'abondance des nuances du mobilier choisi quant aux modèles, couleurs et textures.

Material und Farben wurden ganz bewusst reduziert. Als Kontrast bieten die Möbel in Formen, Farben und Mustern mehr Abwechslung.

The bright, open, and functional spaces are enhanced by the color of the decorative elements and the simplicity of the furniture. The result is an unfussy visual richness.

Les espaces vastes, ouverts et fonctionnels sont mis en relief par la couleur des éléments décoratifs et par la simplicité du mobilier. Il en résulte une richesse visuelle ponctuée de simplicité.

Die hellen, offenen, funktionellen Räume bestechen durch die farbenprächtigen Dekorationen und die schlichten Möbel.

The interiors are characterized by order, functionality, and contemporary esthetics. This serene atmosphere makes work a pleasure.

Les intérieurs déclinent ordre, fonctionnalité et esthétique contemporaine. C'est un plaisir que de travailler dans cette atmosphère sereine.

Das Innere zeichnet sich durch Ordnung, Funktionalität und moderne Ästhetik aus. In dieser Atmosphäre wird Arbeit zum Vergnügen.

The use of translucent dividers manages to isolate a space while at the same time affording visual communication and lightness.

L'emploi de cloisons translucides permet d'isoler l'espace, lui conférant en même temps communication visuelle et légèreté.

Die durchscheinenden Trennelemente isolieren Bereiche und sorgen gleichzeitig für optischen Zusammenhang und Helligkeit.

☐ Unified Fields

Hariri & Hariri Architecture

The premises of Unified Fields, a company in the multimedia and software design business, are located in New York City's Silicon Alley, one of the most dynamic regions of the city in terms of economy. The Hariri & Hariri Architecture studio was commissioned to design a new space that faithfully reflects the activities of the company. The resulting workplace had to allow the team of programmers, designers, and collaborators to carry out their tasks as comfortably as possible, in a relaxed and modern atmosphere with innovative and engaging esthetics. In keeping with the client's brief, the space was planned following the design principles for a loft: large, bright, continuous, open areas that have been given an industrial treatment. The work zones were organized in small spaces, giving the occupants a sense of privacy, even though they are in an open and common area that encourages communication. The lighting and materials emphasize the modern, industrial feel.

Les locaux de Unified Fields, une compagnie de multimédia et de design de logiciel, se situent dans la Silicon Alley de New York City, une des zones les plus dynamiques de la cité sur le plan économique. Le studio d'architecture Hariri & Hariri a été chargé de concevoir un nouvel espace reflétant fidèlement les activités de l'entreprise. Le futur espace de bureaux doit permettre aux programmateurs, designers et collaborateurs de travailler dans un cadre aussi confortable que possible, dans une atmosphère moderne et relaxante à l'esthétique innovante et dynamique. A la requête du client, l'espace a été conçu selon les principes de design d'un loft : surfaces larges, fluides et ouvertes dotées du flair des bâtiments industriels. Les zones de travail sont organisées en petits espaces, conférant aux occupants une certaine sensation d'intimité, même dans des aires ouvertes et communes propices à la communication. L'éclairage et les matériaux exaltent la modernité du site industriel.

Die Büroräume von Unified Fields, einem Unternehmen der Multimedia- und Softwaredesign-Industrie, befinden sich in der Silicon Alley in New York City. Das Architekturstudio Hariri & Hariri wurde mit dem Entwurf beauftragt. Der daraus entstandene Arbeitsbereich sollte es dem Team von Programmierern, Designern und Mitarbeitern ermöglichen, ihre Aufgaben in einer entspannten und modern anmutenden Atmosphäre mit einer innovativen und Energie geladenen Ästhetik so bequem wie möglich auszuführen. Um den Vorgaben des Kunden zu entsprechen, wurde der Raum nach den Designgrundlagen für ein Loft ausgelegt: Weite, Helligkeit, durchgängige, offene Flächen, die dennoch gewerblich angehaucht sind. Die Arbeitsbereiche wurden in kleine Räume unterteilt und bieten so den Mitarbeitern ein Gefühl von Privatsphäre, obwohl sie sich alle in einem offenen und gemeinsam genutzten Bereich aufhalten. Die Beleuchtung und das Material unterstützen das moderne, gewerbliche Ambiente.

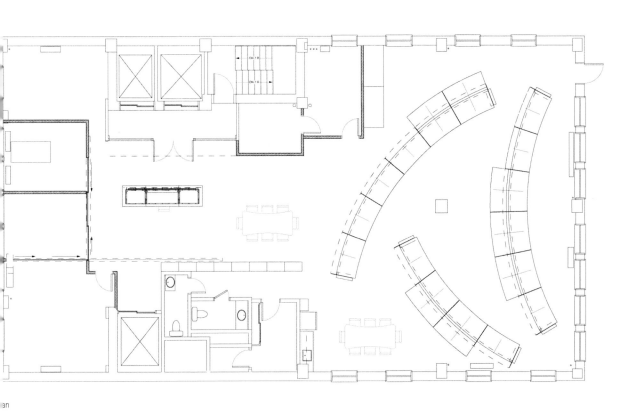

an

Grouping the work areas in a single curvilinear module presents numerous advantages, as well as creating an additional decorative element.

Le regroupement de plusieurs zones dans un module aux lignes courbes offre de nombreux avantages et ajoute un élément décoratif.

Die Anordnung der Arbeitsbereiche in einem freihstehend, gebogenen Modul bietet viele Vorteile und ist gleichzeitig dekorativ.

The design sought to achieve flexible, dynamic, practical, and functional spaces where work could be carried out as comfortably as possible.

Le design des espaces devait être flexible, dynamique, pratique et fonctionnel pour que le travail puisse se réaliser dans les meilleures conditions d'ambiance et de confort.

Ziel war es, flexible, dynamische, praktische und funktionelle Räume zu schaffen und eine angenehme Arbeitsumgebung zu erzeugen.

The reception area includes a table-counter with straight lines and translucent sliding panels to the rear that mask the meeting room and multimedia rooms.

La zone de réception comprend une table comptoir aux lignes droites et des panneaux coulissants à l'arrière pour masquer la salle de conférence et les pièces multimédias.

Hinter dem Empfangsbereich mit geradlinigem Tresen und durchscheinenden Schiebewänden liegen Konferenzsaal und Multimedia-Raum.

☐ Fred

Oskar Leo Kaufmann

Fred is an expandable unit measuring 10 by 10 by 10 ft when closed and stretching up to 710 ft when fully extended on its rails. This is possible thanks to its design, incorporating walls that slide in response to electronic controls. The interior is used as a workspace with a rest room and kitchenette. Fred's versatility, lightness, and compactness–when closed–make it easy to transport and relocate. Once in position, the unit just needs to be hooked up to the utilities and electronically opened to be ready for use. A strong, sturdy structure was needed to withstand a lot of movement, so high-quality, well-built, precision materials were used. The wooden framework used in the sections and the opening/closing system is completely covered by colored plywood panels, and the entrance boasts a large window. Furnishings and other accessories needed for office operations are built into the unit, making Fred ideal for businesses on the go.

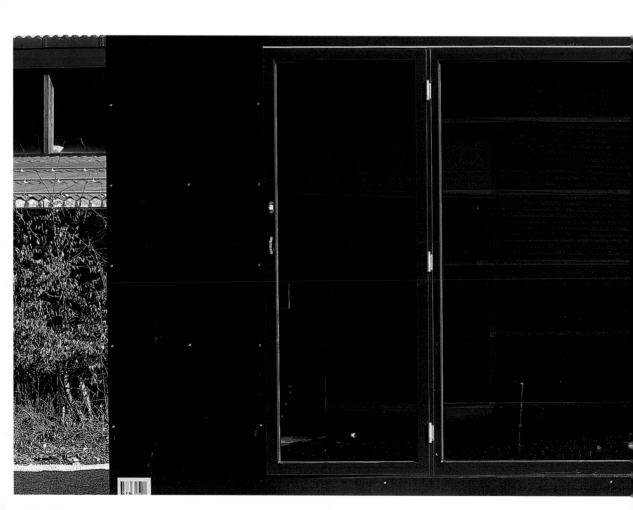

Fred est une unité extensible qui, fermée, mesure 3 m sur 3 m et peut aller jusqu'à 216 m, une fois entièrement étirée sur ses rails. Ceci grâce à un design de murs coulissants commandés électroniquement. L'intérieur sert d'espace de bureau doté d'une salle de repos et d'une kitchenette. L'aspect modulable, léger et compact de Fred –quand il est fermé– facilite son transport et sa réinstallation. Une fois en place, il suffit d'ancrer l'unité et d'enclencher le système électronique pour qu'elle fonctionne. Soumise à de nombreux déplacements, il a fallu renforcer sa résistance par des matériaux solides conjuguant précision et haute qualité. Le châssis en bois, utilisé dans les cloisons et dans le système d'ouverture et de fermeture, est entièrement revêtu de panneaux colorés en contreplaqué, et l'entrée est parée d'une grande fenêtre. Meubles et autres accessoires nécessaires pour le bureau sont intégrés à l'unité, faisant de Fred la formule idéale pour des affaires qui marchent!

Fred ist eine ausziehbare Einheit, die im geschlossenen Zustand 3x3x3 m misst und bis auf 216 m ausziehbar ist. Das Innere kann als Arbeitsraum mit einem WC und einer Kochnische genutzt werden. Freds Vielseitigkeit, Helligkeit und –im geschlossenen Zustand– Kompaktheit machen es zu einem ausgesprochen mobilen Arbeitsplatz. Sobald Fred in Position gerollt wird, muss die Einheit nur an die Versorgungsleitungen angeschlossen und elektronisch geöffnet werden und ist sofort einsatzbereit. Es wurden nur qualitativ hochwertige, gut gebaute Präzisionsmaterialien verwendet. Das hölzerne Rahmenwerk, das für die einzelnen Bereiche und das Verschlusssystem verwendet wurde, ist komplett von farbigen Sperrholzplatten umgeben. Im Eingang gibt es ein großes Fenster. Die Ausstattung und andere Accessoires für den Bürobetrieb sind direkt in die Einheit mit eingebaut und machen Fred so zum idealen mobilen Büro.

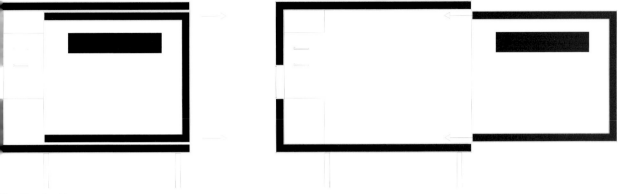

Plans Plans Grundrisse

When the new location was chosen, the ground was leveled, the base was put in place, and the rails were positioned.
Le socle a été posé et les rails mis en place, une fois l'emplacement choisi et le sol nivelé.
Nach der Wahl des neuen Standorts wurde der Boden geebnet, und die Basis und die Schienen wurden platziert.

The inner box slides out over two rails on the bottom of the unit, doubling the amount of interior space.

La boite intérieure glisse sur les deux rails installés sur le sol de l'unité, doublant ainsi la surface de l'espace intérieur.

Die innere Box gleitet über zwei Schienen an der Unterseite und verdoppelt so den Platz im Inneren.

☐ TBWA/Chiat/Day

Marmol Radziner + Associates

The client approached the architecture studio of Marmol Radziner + Associates with a clear brief for a creative, warm, modern, and visually striking space for the offices of the TBWA/Chiat/Day agency in San Francisco, California. Since the structure of the existing building was preserved, including its brick walls, wooden ceilings and columns, the project began with a head start. An open space was created to take advantage of all these elements and connect the various areas and departments in a fluid, natural way. A large, curved wooden structure is the element that defines and connects the first and second levels. It is a striking curvilinear volume of unquestionable visual power that serves to distribute the space. The furniture has been carefully selected and is arranged to create several informal, cozy, relaxed, and modern spaces where ideas can flow freely and work becomes a pleasure.

Le client a chargé le studio d'architecture Marmol Radziner + Associates de créer un espace, original, chaleureux, moderne et à fort impact visuel pour les bureaux de l'agence TBWA/Chiat/Day à San Francisco, en Californie. La structure existante préservée, y compris les murs en briques, les plafonds de bois et les colonnes, a permis au projet de démarrer vite. Pour tirer parti de tous ces éléments, l'espace a été ouvert, connectant les diverses zones et services de manière fluide et naturelle. Une grande structure de bois incurvée, définit et relie le premier étage au deuxième. C'est un volume aux lignes incurvées d'une puissance visuelle absolument fabuleuse qui permet de distribuer l'espace. Le mobilier, sélectionné avec le plus grand soin, est modulable pour créer diverses zones informelles, confortables, relaxantes et modernes où les idées peuvent s'épanouir librement et où travailler est un véritable plaisir.

Der Kunde ist an das Architekturstudio Marmos Radziner + Associates herangetreten und bat um einen kreativen, warmen, modernen und visuell ansprechenden Entwurf für die Büroräume der Agentur TBWA/Chiat/Day in San Francisco. Da die Struktur des bestehenden Gebäudes inklusive ihrer Ziegelwände, Holzdecken und Säulen beibehalten wurde, konnte das Projekt schon bald aufgenommen werden. Ein offener Raum wurde geschaffen, um all diese Elemente mit einzubeziehen und gleichzeitig die verschiedenen Bereiche und Abteilungen auf natürliche Art und Weise miteinander zu verbinden. Eine lange, gebogene Holzstruktur grenzt die erste und zweite Etage voneinander ab. Es handelt sich dabei um ein beeindruckendes kurvig-lineares Gerüst, das den Raum klar unterteilt. Das Mobiliar wurde sorgfältig ausgesucht und so arrangiert, dass verschiedene ungezwungene, gemütliche, entspannte und moderne Räume geschaffen wurden, in denen Ideen wachsen können und die Arbeit zum Vergnügen wird.

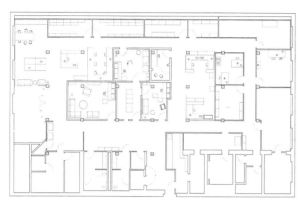

Ground floor Rez-de-chaussée Erdgeschoss

First floor Premier étage Erstes Obergeschoss

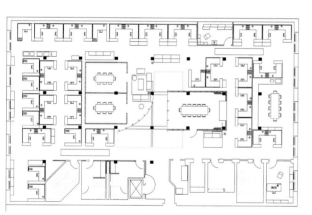

Second floor Deuxième étage Zweite Obergeschoss

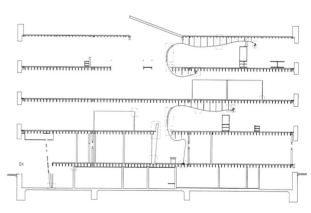

Longitudinal section Section longitudinale Längsschnitt

A large, curved wooden structure is the element that defines and connects the first and second levels.

Une grande structure de bois incurvée défini les deux niveaux qu'elle relie entre eux.

Eine lange, gebogene Holzstruktur verbindet das erste und zweite Stockwerk miteinander und grenzt die Ebenen ab.

The sinuous movement of the wooden element unfolds vertically to delineate the ceiling of the second floor, encompassing a distinctive conference room.
Le mouvement sinueux de l'élément en bois se déroule à la verticale pour délimiter le plafond du deuxième étage et créer une salle de conférence.
Die wellenförmige Bewegung des Holzelements verläuft vertikal bis zur Decke der zweiten Etage und umgibt den Konferenzraum.

The choice of wood as one of the main materials, the clever combination of colors, and the successful handling of light helped to create interiors that are well-balanced, warm, and flowing.

Le choix du bois comme l'un des matériaux essentiels, l'agencement astucieux des couleurs et un éclairage réussi ont contribué à la création d'intérieurs harmonieux, chaleureux et fluides.

Das Holz, die Farbkombination und die gelungene Beleuchtungslösung schaffen eine ausgeglichene, warme, fließende Umgebung.

☐ No Picnic

Claesson Koivisto Rune Arkitektkontor

The architectural studio Claesson, Koivisto and Rune were hired to transform an industrial building from the 1930s into the headquarters of the Swedish industrial design company No Picnic. The company's creative character inspired the architects to come up with a dynamic, open space that also provides intimate areas where projects could be developed in privacy. The space was divided vertically into three levels: the basement for the technical section, the entrance level for the rooms used by all the staff members—the reception, kitchen, meeting rooms and workshop—and finally, the floor above for the more secluded project room. Despite the clearly defined layout, the architects saw the project as a maze, and this approach is reflected in the way the staircase articulates the spaces, defines the levels and separates the workshop from the communal rooms. The double-height ceiling adds to the room's luminosity and recalls the building's industrial past.

Le bureau d'architecture Claesson, Koivisto et Rune a été engagé pour transformer un bâtiment industriel des années 30, en siège social de la compagnie suédoise de design industriel No Picnic. Influencés par l'élan novateur de cette compagnie, les architectes ont créé un espace ouvert et dynamique doté aussi de zones privées plus intimes, propices à l'étude et à la création de projets. L'espace, divisé à la verticale, englobe trois niveaux : le sous-sol pour le service technique, le niveau d'accès pour les pièces communes —réception, cuisine, salles de réunions et atelier— et finalement, l'étage supérieur pour les salles de projet plus retirées. Forts d'un concept clairement défini, les architectes ont traité ce projet à l'instar d'un labyrinthe. Approche qui se reflète dans l'articulation de l'espace autour de l'escalier : définition des niveaux et séparation de l'atelier des pièces communes. La double hauteur de plafond accentue la luminosité de la pièce et rappelle le passé industriel du bâtiment.

Das Architekturstudio Claesson, Kovisto & Rune wurde damit beauftragt, ein gewerblich genutztes Gebäude aus den 30er Jahren in die Hauptgeschäftsstelle des schwedischen Industriedesignerunternehmens No Picnic umzuwandeln. Es wurde ein dynamischer, offener Raum geschaffen, der aber auch Räume enthält, in denen einzelne Projekte in Ruhe bearbeitet werden können. Der Raum wurde vertikal in drei Ebenen unterteilt: Der Keller für den technischen Bereich, die Eingangsebene für die Gemeinschaftsräume —Rezeption, Küche, Meetingräume und Workshops— und die obere Etage für die eher privaten Projekträume. Trotz eindeutig definiertem Layout haben die Architekten das Projekt eher als ein Puzzle konzipiert, was sich besonders in der Form äußert, wie das Treppenhaus die einzelnen Flächen voneinander abgrenzt. Die extrem hohen Decken tragen zur Helligkeit des Raumes bei und erinnern an die industriell genutzte Vergangenheit des Gebäudes.

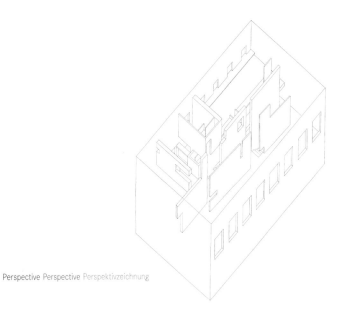

Perspective Perspective Perspektivzeichnung

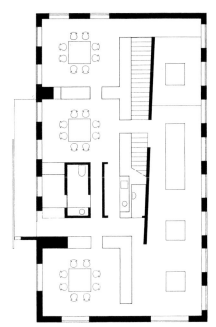

Lower level Niveau inférieur Untere Ebene

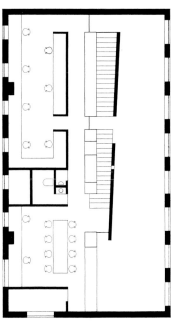

Upper level Niveau supérireur Obere Ebene

Geometric openings have been cut into the partition walls and covered by sheets of colored glass.

Des ouvertures géométriques sont découpées dans les cloisons et recouvertes de couches de verre coloré.

In den Trennwänden befinden sich geometrische Öffnungen, die mit farbigen Glasscheiben abgedeckt sind.

part from the open-plan layout, the firm also required more intimate spaces where projects could be developed in privacy.

la requête de l'entreprise, l'espace doit être ouvert mais être aussi complété par des pièces plus intimes pour l'étude de projets dans un cadre plus privé.

eben Großraumbüros benötigte das Unternehmen auch abgeteilte Räume mit mehr Privatsphäre zur Entwicklung neuer Projekte.

☐ International Sports Agency

Aurora Cuito + Alejandro Bahamón

These offices in downtown Barcelona house an international sports agency that was seeking for more flexibility on its 600 sq. ft premises. The renovation unified the original space by removing the existing partitions and dividing the space in a direction perpendicular to the office's only windows, taking the fullest advantage of the available natural light. A natural wood floor helps to make the space feel like a cohesive whole, while orange is used to provide emphatic touches on some of the furnishings and on the wall separating the two main areas. Glass doors on either side of this central wall provide transparent sound insulation and emphasize the wall's prominence. The furnishings enhance flexibility while providing another unifying element. The orange elements attached to the walls are fixed modules that serve as work and storage surfaces, while the white elements can be changed to suit the needs of the staff.

Ces bureaux du centre de Barcelone hébergent une agence de sport international, recherchant plus de flexibilité pour ses locaux de 55 m². La rénovation a unifié l'espace en ôtant les cloisons existantes et en le divisant perpendiculairement aux fenêtres du bureau, bénéficiant ainsi au maximum de la lumière naturelle. Le plancher de bois contribue à unifier l'ensemble de l'espace, ponctué de quelques touches d'orange sur certains meubles et sur les murs, pour séparer les deux zones principales. Des portes vitrées de chaque côté de ce mur central isolent du bruit et soulignent l'importance du mur. L'ameublement accentue la flexibilité et contribue à unifier l'ensemble. Les éléments oranges accrochés aux murs sont des modules fixes et font office de plan de travail ou d'espace de rangement. Les éléments blancs peuvent être modifiés au gré des besoins du personnel.

Diese Büroräume in der Innenstadt von Barcelona beherbergen eine internationale Sportagentur, die nach mehr Flexibilität für die 55 qm Fläche suchte. Bei der Neugestaltung wurde der ursprüngliche Raum vergrößert, die bestehenden Trennwände entfernt und der Raum im rechten Winkel zum einzigen Fenster unterteilt, um das natürliche Tageslicht auszunutzen. Ein natürlicher Holzboden sorgt dafür, dass der Raum in sich ruht, während mit der Farbe Orange einzelne Elemente der Ausstattung und die Trennwand zwischen den beiden Hauptbereichen betont wurden. Glastüren auf beiden Seiten dieser Mittelwand sorgen für transparenten Lärmschutz. Die Ausstattung bietet die erforderliche Flexibilität und dient gleichzeitig als verbindendes Element. Die orangefarbenen Elemente an den Wänden sind feste Module, die sowohl als Arbeits- als auch Lagerflächen dienen, während die weißen Elemente, je nach Anforderungen der Mitarbeiter, ausgetauscht werden können.

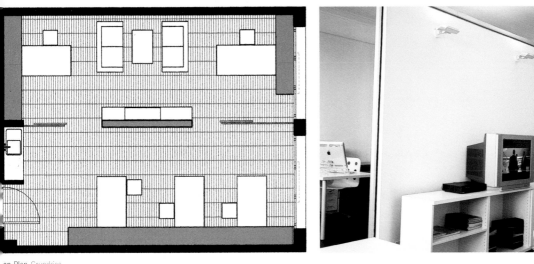

an Plan Grundriss

The space was divided in a direction perpendicular to the office's only windows, thus taking full advantage of the available natural light.
L'espace est divisé perpendiculairement en fonction des seules fenêtres du bureau, bénéficiant totalement de la lumière du jour naturelle disponible.
Der Raum wurde rechtwinklig zur einzigen Fensterfront unterteilt um das Tageslicht optimal auszunutzen.

In the workers' area, desks can be added, removed, or combined in accordance with the agency's needs.

Dans la zone de travail, il est possible d'ajouter, d'enlever ou de combiner les bureaux au gré des besoins de l'agence.

Die Schreibtische können je nach Bedarf verschoben oder kombiniert werden, oder es können neue hinzugefügt werden.

☐ Puig NY

GCA Arquitectos

GCA Architectos was commissioned to refurbish the headquarters of the Catalan perfume company, Puig, located on the 26th floor of a building in central New York. Designed on the premise of neutral and fluid environments, the project consisted of a reception, two meeting rooms, two board rooms, offices, secretarial offices, an archive area and a small kitchen. After leaving the elevators and staircases, two large glass doors usher visitors into the haven of simplicity and clarity lying on the other side. The reception and the secretarial area are situated in an open space, while the meeting rooms are placed on the perimeter, to take advantage of the natural light flowing in through the large windows. The construction methods and materials and the use of recurring textures and colors throughout the premises provides the homogeneity that was an essential requisite of the project from the outset.

Le bureau d'architecture GCA Architectos a été chargé de réno-ver le siège social de la société catalane de parfums, Puig, située au 26e étage d'un bâtiment au centre de New York. Conçu dans un contexte environnemental fluide et neutre, le projet comprend une réception, deux salles de conférence, deux salles de direction, des bureaux, des secrétariats, une zone d'archives et une petite cuisine. Après avoir quitté les ascenseurs et les escaliers, deux grandes portes vitrées intro-duisent les visiteurs dans un havre de simplicité et de clarté, situé de l'autre côté. La réception et le secrétariat sont dans un espace ouvert, les salles de conférence situées sur le périmèt-re, bénéficient ainsi des flots de lumière naturelle inondant les grandes fenêtres. Les méthodes de construction, les matériaux et l'emploi général de textures et couleurs récurrentes, répon-dent au critère essentiel d'homogénéité fixé d'emblée par le projet.

GCA Architectos wurde mit der Neugestaltung der Hauptge-schäftsstelle der katalonischen Parfümhersteller Puig beauf-tragt, die sich auf der 26. Etage eines Gebäudes im Herzen New Yorks befindet. Das Projekt wurde mit der Prämisse einer neu-tralen und fließenden Umgebung gestaltet und besteht aus einer Rezeption, zwei Konferenzräumen, zwei Räumen für die Geschäftsleitung, Sekretariat, einem Archiv und einer kleinen Küche. Hinter dem Treppenhaus und den Fahrstühlen laden zwei große Glastüren die Besucher in die eigentlichen Geschäftsräume ein. Die Rezeption und das Sekretariat sind in einem offenen Raum angesiedelt, während die Konferenzräume im rechten Winkel dazu liegen, um das durch die großen Fens-ter einfallende Tageslicht zu nutzen. Die Baumethoden, die Materialien und der Einsatz von sich wiederholenden Texturen und Farben im gesamten Bereich unterstützen die Homogenität, eine der essentiellen Requisiten bei diesem Projekt.

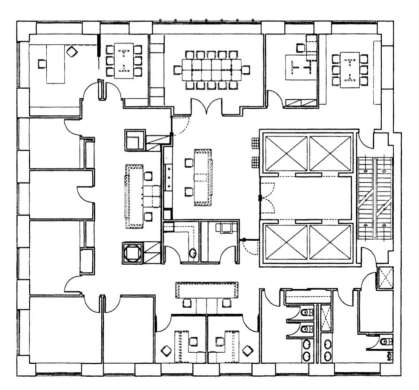

Plan Plan Grundriss

The headquarters of the Catalan perfume company Puig were set up on the 26th floor of a skyscraper in central New York.

Le siège social de la société catalane de parfum Puig est installé au 26e étage d'un gratte-ciel, au centre de New York.

Im 26. Stock eines Wolkenkratzers im Herzen von New York wurde der Hauptsitz der katalanischen Parfümerie Puig eingerichtet.

The maple wood, stainless steel and black leather used in the interior design endow the office with a sober and homogenous image, as well as a warm atmosphere.

L'alliance de bois d'érable, d'acier et de cuir noir qui définit le design intérieur, confère au bureau une image sobre et homogène dotée d'une atmosphère chaleureuse.

Ahorn, Edelstahl und schwarzes Leder geben dem Inneren eine nüchterne, homogene Note und schaffen gleichzeitig eine warme Atmosphäre.

The offices and the meeting rooms are placed at the perimeter of the floor. This guarantees that they enjoy abundant natural light flowing in from the large windows, opened in the walls

Les bureaux et les salles de réunion sont placés sur le périmètre de l'étage. Ce qui leur permet de bénéficier d'une abondante lumière naturelle venant des grandes baies vitrées.

Büros und Konferenzräume liegen außen und werden von Tageslicht durchflutet, das durch die großen Fenster einfällt.

☐ Acacia Tours

Interior Designer: Marta Ortega Batlle

The main objective of this project was to adapt approximately 1,291 sq. ft. of commercial space into offices for a travel agency. The interior designer Marta Ortega Batlle drew up a neutral, perfectly organized space, where the independent vertical planes made of wood, plasterboard, and screens define the different functions of the agency, such as the administrative areas, customer service, storage, and offices. In the lobby, visitors are welcomed by two large screens bearing the logo of the agency. These are located behind a large counter whose height affords a view of the activity within. In order to isolate the administrative area from the exterior without any loss of light, movable dividers and display panels were installed; these modify the perception of space according to whether they are open or closed. Such strategies contributed to the creation of a balanced, restrained, and highly functional space where customers come to plan their dream vacations.

L'objectif principal de ce projet est de transformer les 120 m² d'un espace commercial, en bureaux pour une agence de voyage. Marta Ortega Batlle, designer d'intérieur, a conçu un espace neutre, parfaitement organisé où les plans verticaux indépendants, fait de bois, de placoplâtre et d'écrans, définissent les différentes fonctions de l'agence : zones administratives, service clientèle, magasin et bureau. Dans le lobby, les visiteurs sont accueillis par deux grands écrans portant le logo de l'agence, situés derrière un grand comptoir dont la taille permet d'apercevoir ce qui s'y passe. Des cloisons amovibles et des écrans ont été installés afin d'isoler la zone administrative de l'extérieur, sans perte de lumière. Fermés ou ouverts, ils modifient la perception de l'espace. De telles stratégies permettent de créer un espace harmonieux, restreint et hautement fonctionnel ou les clients viennent planifier leurs vacances de rêve.

Hauptziel dieses Projektes war es die, ca. 120 m² Gewerbefläche in Büroräume eines Reisebüros zu verwandeln. Die Innenarchitektin Marta Ortega Battle hat einen neutralen, perfekt organisierten Raum entworfen, in dem die voneinander unabhängigen, senkrechten Wände aus Holz, Gipsplatten und Glas die einzelnen Funktionen der Agentur voneinander abgrenzen. In der Lobby werden die Besucher von zwei großen Bildschirmen mit dem Logo der Agentur willkommen geheißen. Um den Verwaltungsbereich nach außen hin ohne Einbußen an Licht abzugrenzen, wurden bewegliche Trennwände und Anzeigetafeln installiert. Diese können individuell das Gefühl von Raum variieren. Derartige Strategien trugen zur Schaffung eines ausgewogenen, in sich abgegrenzten und dennoch ausgesprochen funktionellen Raumes bei, in dem die Kunden ihren Traumurlaub planen können.

The strict and controlled palette of materials (wood, steel, plasterboard, and glass) contributes to the main objectives of the project - balance and pragmatism.

La palette sobre et bien définie de matériaux (bois, acier, placoplâtre et verre) répond aux critères essentiels du projet - équilibre et pragmatisme.

Die beschränkte Palette an verwendetem Material (Holz, Stahl, Gipstafeln und Glas) trägt zu Ausgewogenheit und Pragmatismus bei.

The depth of the space is defined by a plasterboard wall with the name of the agency displayed in steel letters, thus restricting the visual access to the more private areas of the office.

La profondeur de l'espace est définie par un mur en placoplâtre portant le nom de l'agence en lettres d'acier. Il limite l'accès visuel aux zones plus privées du bureau.

Hinter einer Trennwand aus Gipstafeln, auf der der Firmenname in Stahlbuchstaben geschrieben steht, liegen die nicht öffentlichen Bereiche.

☐ **Xavier Martín Studio**

Xavier Martín

The new Xavier Martín studio, located on a central street in Mataró, a city near Barcelona, Spain, is a multifunctional space that occupies approximately 969 sq. ft. of the lower level of an early-twentieth-century building. The studio, which specializes in architecture, interior design, and furniture design, was directly responsible for redesigning its own premises. The aim of the refurbishment was to remove the partition walls to create a larger, more fluid space free of visual interruptions. A large, stainless-steel door adorned with the company's logo leads to the offices. The oak table designed by the studio, the sinuous Panton chairs, and the filing cabinet with simple lines welcome the visitor into the space. All the work areas share the same space, except for a private office enclosed in glass with an automatic door. The patio, set at the rear of the premises, has been renovated and incorporated into the interior.

Le nouveau studio, Xavier Martín, situé sur une avenue centrale de Mataró, ville près de Barcelone, en Espagne, est un espace polyvalent qui occupe environ les 90 m² du niveau inférieur d'un bâtiment du début du XXe siècle. Le studio, spécialisé en architecture, design d'intérieur et mobilier design, a restauré ses propres locaux. La rénovation prévoyait de supprimer les cloisons pour créer un espace plus grand, plus fluide et libéré de tout écran visuel. Une grande porte en acier, décorée du logo de l'entreprise, s'ouvre sur les bureaux. La table en chêne conçue par le studio, les chaises sinueuses de Panton et l'armoire à dossiers aux lignes épurées, accueillent le visiteur dans cet univers design. Les bureaux partagent tous le même espace, à l'exception d'un bureau privé, entouré d'un écrin de verre et doté d'une porte automatique. A l'arrière du local, le patio, rénové, s'intègre à l'espace intérieur.

Das neue Studio Xavier Martín auf der Hauptstraße in Mataró, einem Vorort von Barcelona, ist ein multifunktioneller Raum, der etwa 90 m² der unteren Ebene eines Gebäudes aus dem frühen 20. Jh. belegt. Das Studio, das sich auf Architektur, Innenausstattung und Möbeldesign spezialisiert hat, entwarf die neuen Büroräume selbst. Ziel der Neugestaltung war es, die Trennwände zu entfernen, um einen weiteren, durchgängigeren Raum, frei von visuellen Unterbrechungen zu schaffen. Eine große Tür aus Edelstahl mit dem Logo des Unternehmens führt in die Büroräume. Der Eichentisch, der von dem Studio selbst entworfen wurde, die gewundenen Panton-Stühle und der Ablageschrank mit seiner klaren Linienführung heißen den Besucher willkommen. Alle Arbeitsbereiche teilen sich den selben Raum. Die Ausnahme bildet ein privates Glasbüro mit einer automatischen Tür. Der Innenhof, der hinter den Büroräumen liegt, wurde neu gestaltet und in den Innenraum mit einbezogen.

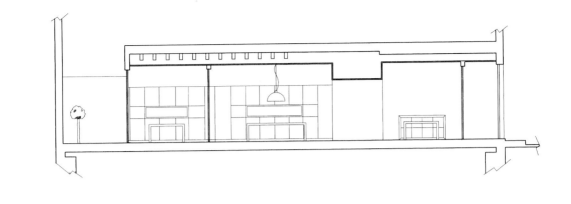

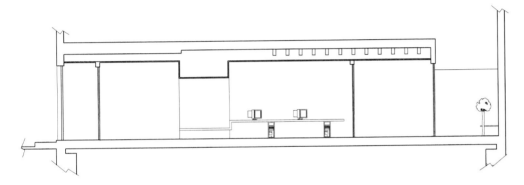

Sections Sections Schnitte

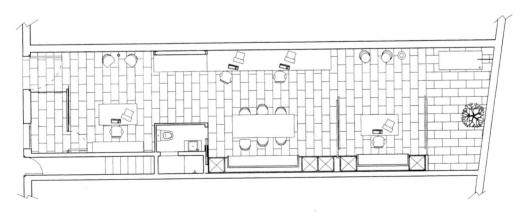

Plan Plan Grundriss

Following the guidelines used for traditional lofts, a single space was created with the various areas defined by the distribution of furnishings and the insertion of glass dividers.

Dans la tradition du loft, meubles et cloisons en verre sont répartis dans l'espace unique pour en définir les différentes zones.

Wie bei einem Loft wurde ein einziger Raum mit verschiedenen durch Möbel und Glaswände abgeteilten Bereichen geschaffen.

A private office is enclosed in glass with an automatic door, which can be quickly closed from view when necessary.

Un bureau privé est inséré dans un écrin de verre fermé par une porte automatique. Le cas échéant, l'ensemble peut être rapidement protégé des regards extérieurs.

Ein abgeschlossenes Büro mit Glaswänden und Automatiktür kann bei Bedarf gegen Blicke von außen geschützt werden.

☐ British Summer

Archikubik

This office, located in Barcelona, Spain, accommodates a company that sells courses abroad for children and adults and seeks to transmit a strong public image. Several design strategies were brought together to create an interesting interplay of spaces, from the entrance right back to the workstations. An interaction with an urban flavor is established by the polycarbonate lighting used in the entrance area, and various settings are created by changing the colors of the fluorescent lights as they recede. In this way, the business's presence is signaled to passer-by in a striking manner without falling back on external elements like banners. The play of geometric shapes, the large public service area, and the lack of clutter all help to effectively attract the public's attention. The play of colors changes with the time of day and season of the year: yellow for day, blue for night, red for summer, purple for winter, and so forth.

Ce bureau, implanté à Barcelone en Espagne, héberge une compagnie qui vend des cours à l'étranger pour enfants et adultes et qui cherche à transmettre au public une forte image de marque. Plusieurs stratégies ont été réunies pour créer un jeu d'espaces intéressant, de l'entrée jusqu'aux bureaux. Dans cet esprit, l'éclairage en poly carbonate de l'entrée apporte une touche urbaine, à laquelle s'ajoute une mise en scène de couleurs fluorescentes qui changent à tour de rôle. C'est une façon originale d'attirer l'attention du passant sur l'activité professionnelle, sans avoir recours à des enseignes publicitaires extérieures. Le jeu de formes géométriques, la grande aire de services publics et la clarté de l'espace contribuent efficacement à attirer l'attention du public. Le jeu de couleurs varie selon le moment de la journée et la saison de l'année : jaune pour le jour, bleu pour la nuit, rouge pour l'été, violet pour l'hiver, et ainsi de suite.

Dieses Büro in Barcelona betreibt ein Unternehmen, das Kurse für Kinder und Erwachsene im Ausland verkauft und ein nachhaltiges, öffentliches Image zu vermitteln sucht. Es wurden verschiedene Designstrategien miteinander verbunden, um ein interessantes Zusammenspiel der einzelnen Räume zu schaffen. Dem städtischen Charakter wurde durch die Polykarbonat-Beleuchtung im Eingangsbereich Vorschub geleistet und verschiedene Stimmungen wurden durch farbiges, fluoreszierendes Licht geschaffen. Auf diese Weise zieht das Büro die Aufmerksamkeit der vorbeigehenden Fußgänger auf sich, ohne unbedingt auf externe Werbeflächen zurückgreifen zu müssen. Das Spiel mit geometrischen Formen, der große öffentliche Servicebereich und das Fehlen überflüssigen Ballastes ziehen die Aufmerksamkeit des Publikums auf sich. Das Farbspiel ändert sich im Laufe des Tages und der Jahreszeiten: gelb am Tag, blau bei Nacht, rot im Sommer, lila im Winter, und so weiter.

he high table, chairs with rollers, and furnishings that are suspended or flush with the walls set up an uninterrupted view of the floor, enhancing the feeling of spaciousness.

a table surélevée, les chaises sur roulettes et les meubles suspendus ou intégrés aux murs, dégagent la vue au sol exaltant la sensation d'espace.

er hohe Tisch, Stühle mit Rollen und hängende oder in die Wand integrierte Möbel sorgen für ein Gefühl der Geräumigkeit.

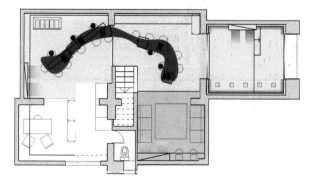

Ground floor Rez-de-chaussée Erdgeschoss

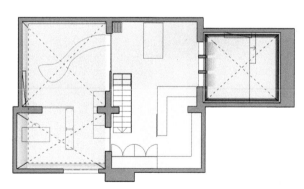

First floor Premier étage Erstes Obergeschoss

he play of colors changes with the time of day or season of the year: yellow for day, blue for night, red for summer, purple for winter, and so forth.

e jeu de couleurs varie selon l'heure de la journée ou la saison de l'année : jaune pour le jour, bleu pour la nuit, rouge pour l'été, pourpre pour l'hiver et ainsi de suite.

as Farbspiel wechselt je nach Tages- oder Jahreszeit: Gelb für den Tag, Blau für den Abend, Rot für Sommer, Lila für Winter und so weiter.

An interaction with an urban flavor is established by the polycarbonate lighting used in the entrance area.

L'éclairage en poly carbonate, utilisé à l'entrée, apporte une touche urbaine.

Durch das Polykarbonatlicht im Eingangsbereich wird eine Verbindung zum urbanen Ambiente geschaffen.

☐ MTV Networks

Felderman & Keatinge Associates

The architectural challenge of designing the new headquarters for MTV Networks was the creation of a space that would fit into an urban setting and, at the same time, stand out as an advertising statement. One of the requirements was a lobby whose structure would relate to the ocean and the surrounding vegetation. The solution was to create a plaza with sand-colored flooring that projects into the lobby and echoes the doorways of the older buildings nearby, as well as blurring the division between outdoors and indoors. A 1957 aluminum trailer welcomes visitors and serves as a waiting room. The pink rug, black-and-white linoleum floors, and Formica kitchen table are just some of the decorative elements inserted to create a '50s flavor. Six television screens were built into the wall next to the trailer and the conference room, fitted out with television sets, rugs, and couches, evokes the atmosphere of a domestic living room.

Créer un espace intégré à l'environnement urbain et en même temps, l'exposer comme une réclame publicitaire, tel est le défi architectural lié à la conception du siège social des MTV Networks. L'idée maîtresse est de construire un lobby dont la structure rappelle l'océan et la végétation environnante. Il a donc été décidé de créer un sol couleur sable qui se projette dans le lobby et rappelle les encadrements de porte de l'ancien bâtiment voisin, tout en estompant la séparation entre l'intérieur et l'extérieur. Une remorque en aluminium, datant de 1957, accueille les visiteurs et fait office de salle d'attente. Le tapis rose, les sols en linoléum noir et blanc et la table de cuisine en formica sont autant d'éléments mis en scène pour donner un air des années 50. Six télévisions sont intégrées dans le mur à côté de la remorque et la salle de conférence, également dotée de télévisions, de tapis et de divans, a des allures de salon privé.

Eine der Prämissen bei der Gestaltung der neuen Hauptgeschäftsräume von MTV Networks war eine Lobby, deren Struktur sich auf das Meer und die umgebende Vegetation beziehen sollte. Man einigte sich auf eine Plaza mit sandfarbenem Boden, bis in die Lobby hineinreicht und die Durchgänge zu den älteren Gebäuden in der Nähe widerspiegelt, gleichzeitig aber auch die Trennung von außen und innen aufhebt. Ein Aluminiumanhänger aus dem Jahr 1957 heißt die Besucher willkommen und dient als Wartezimmer. Die pinkfarbenen Teppiche, schwarz-weiße Linoleumböden und Formica-Küchentische stellen nur einige der dekorativen Elemente dar, mit denen das Ambiente der 50er Jahre nachempfunden werden sollte. Sechs TV-Bildschirme wurden direkt neben den Anhänger in die Wand eingelassen. Das Konferenzzimmer, das mit TV-Geräten, Teppichen und Sofas ausgestattet wurde, ähnelt eher einem gemütlichen Wohnzimmer.

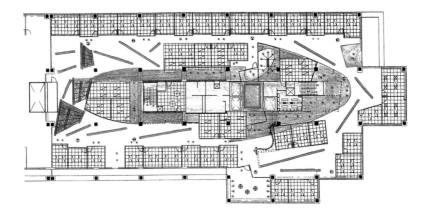

First floor Premier étage Erstes Obergeschoss

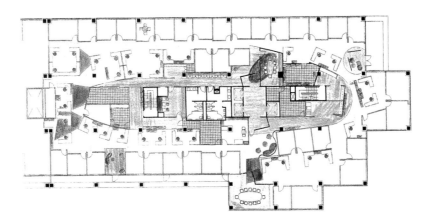

Third floor Troisième étage Dritte Obergeschoss

In the entrance hall, a 1957 aluminum trailer welcomes visitors and serves as a waiting room.

Dans le hall d'entrée, une remorque en aluminium, datant de 1957, accueille les visiteurs et sert de salle d'attente.

In der Eingangshalle heißt ein Aluminiumanhänger aus dem Jahre 1957 die Besucher willkommen, der als Warteraum dient.

The interior combines a stark metal framework with sophisticated coverings, finishes, and materials, such as painted wood, shiny drapes, and glass walls.

L'intérieur conjugue une structure solide en métal et des habillages, finitions et matériaux très raffinés, à l'instar de bois peint, drapés soyeux et mur de verre.

Das Innere beherrschen ein Metallrahmen und ausgefeilte Abdeckungen, Oberflächen sowie Materialien wie Holz, Stoffe und Glaswände.

One of the challenges was the attainment of a structure that relates to the ocean and the surrounding vegetation, so a big bull's eye was inserted into the partition wall in the form of a wave.

L'un des défis à relever était de construire une structure ayant un rapport avec l'océan et la végétation environnante. A cet effet, un immense œil de bœuf en forme de vague, a été percé dans une des cloisons.

Das Bullauge in der wellenförmigen Wand soll eine Verbindung zum Ozean und der Vegetation der Umgebung herstellen.

☐ Montse ...tse ...tse

Stefano Colli

The search for values associated with the type of activity of an esthetic center was an important issue in the conception of this project. In order to create a setting geared to relaxation, health and beauty, the architects made use of materials like stone, mosaics and wood. All of these elements were brought together to represent the world of the senses. In the entrance, a photographic image printed digitally onto vinyl shows a serene and relaxing blue sky with clouds. On the opposite side of the room, a space is reserved for meeting suppliers and for selling cosmetics. A round table, some simple chairs, and a set of light, glass shelves set off the products on display. To take advantage of a free corner, an attractive space was created with a wall mirror and built-in lighting. Outside, the services on offer are repeatedly announced in vinyl lettering on the shop window.

La quête de valeurs inhérentes au type d'activité d'un centre d'esthétique est un critère décisif dans le concept de ce projet. Pour créer une atmosphère consacrée à la relaxation, la santé et la beauté, les architectes ont employé des matériaux tels que la pierre, la mosaïque et le bois. Tous ces éléments ont été réunis pour représenter le monde des sens. A l'entrée, une photo digitale imprimée sur vinyle, montre un ciel serein et apaisant ponctué de nuages. De l'autre côté de la pièce, un espace est réservé aux fournisseurs et à la vente de produits cosmétiques. Une table ronde, des chaises simples et quelques sources lumineuses, ainsi que des étagères de verre mettent en scène les produits exposés. Un coin dégagé accueille un espace agréable doté d'un miroir mural avec éclairage intégré. A l'extérieur, les services offerts sont affichés en lettres de vinyle sur la devanture du magasin.

Die Suche nach Werten, die mit den Aktivitäten eines Schönheitssalons in Einklang zu bringen wären, war eines der herausragenden Themen bei der Konzeption dieses Projektes. Um einen Raum zu schaffen, der sowohl Entspannung, Wellness, aber auch Schönheit widerspiegelt, haben die Architekten Material wie Steine, Mosaike und Holz eingesetzt. All diese Elemente wurden verwendet, um die Sinne anzusprechen. Im Eingangsbereich sorgt ein digital auf Vinyl gedrucktes Foto mit einem wunderschönen blauen Himmel und Wolken direkt für Wohlbefinden und Entspannung. Der Bereich gegenüber bietet Raum für Treffen mit Lieferanten und dem Verkauf von Kosmetik. Ein runder Tisch, einfache Stühle, ein paar Lampen und Glasregale präsentieren die zum verkaufenden Produkte. Um eine freie Ecke effektiv zu nutzen, wurde ein attraktiver Raum mit einem Wandspiegel und eingebauter Beleuchtung geschaffen. Die angebotenen Dienstleistungen werden außen auf dem Schaufenster in Vinylbuchstaben angepriesen.

The forms, materials, textures, and colors succeed in conveying the concepts on which this esthetic center is based - purity and simplicity.

Les formes, les matières, les textures et les couleurs se succèdent, marquées du concept de ce centre esthétique, à savoir pureté et simplicité.

Formen, Materialien, Muster und Farben entsprechen den Konzepten, auf denen ein Schönheitssalon basiert: Reinheit und Schlichtheit.

☐ Adplus Media7 & Werbung AG

Hemmi-Fayet Architects

The challenge of this project was to defy the conventional image associated with the offices of an advertising company and create a modern, transparent, and bright space, without any loss in functionality. The new design only affected one floor, and this is largely of regular proportions. The layout allows for natural and flowing transitions between spaces without ever losing the sense of order. By using white as the main color, the space appears larger and projects reflected light into every corner of the room. The choice of white floors and the soft colors of the furniture forming the partitions define the spaces devoted to different functions. A door with wide, lacquered panels, inserted into a partition wall that separates private and public areas, leads to the entrance of the meeting area. The view of the exterior has only been partially concealed in the main spaces; it is teasingly glimpsed in a subtle, elegant optical game.

Ce projet a pour défi de changer l'image de marque tradition-
nelle des bureaux d'une compagnie publicitaire en créant un
espace moderne, transparent et large sans nuire au fonctionnel.
La nouvelle conception s'applique seulement à un étage, de
proportions très régulières. Le plan permet une transition naturelle et fluide ente les espaces sans jamais perdre le sens de
l'orientation. Le recours au blanc comme couleur principale,
agrandit l'espace et réfléchit la lumière dans tous les coins de
la pièce. Le choix des sols blancs et de couleurs douces pour
les meubles de partition définit les espaces et leurs fonctions.
Une porte dotée de panneaux laqués, intégrés dans une cloison
séparant la partie privée de la partie publique, mène à l'entrée
de l'aire de réunion. La vue sur l'extérieur est partiellement
occultée, dans un jeu de cache-cache optique déclinant subtili-
té et élégance.

Die Herausforderung bei diesem Projekt war es, das konventio-
nelle Image des Unternehmens zu übernehmen und gleichzeitig
einen modernen, transparenten und hellen Raum zu schaffen,
der dennoch nichts an Funktionalität einbüßt. Das Layout
ermöglicht natürliche und fließende Übergänge zwischen den
einzelnen Bereichen, ohne dabei das Gefühl von Ordnung zu
verlieren. Durch den Einsatz der Farbe Weiß als vorherrschende
Farbe wirkt der Raum weiter und heller. Die Wahl von weißen
Böden und sanften Farben bei den Trennmöbeln grenzen die
einzelnen Flächen voneinander ab. Eine Tür mit breiten, lackier-
ten Türblättern, die in eine Trennwand eingebaut wurde, welche
private und öffentliche Bereiche voneinander abgrenzt, führt
zum Eingang des Konferenzbereiches. Die Aussicht im Hauptbereich wurde nur teilweise abgedeckt und damit elegant und sub-
til in ein optisches Spiel verwandelt.

The entrance to the meeting room is a door with wide-lacquered panels set in a glass partition that separates the private and public areas.

L'entrée à la salle de conférence est marquée par une porte dotée de larges panneaux en laque blanche, sertis dans une cloison qui sépare les zones privées et publiques entre elles.

Eingang zum Konferenzraum ist eine weiße Flügeltür in einer Glaswand, die öffentliche und private Zonen voneinander trennt.

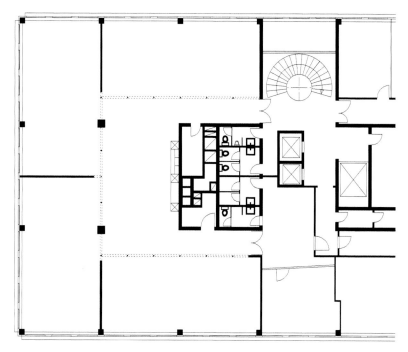

Plan Plan Grundriss

The absence of color on the walls and columns contrasts with the numerous colorful furniture pieces and other decorative elements.

L'absence de couleurs sur les murs et les colonnes contraste avec la richesse du mobilier et de ses coloris ainsi qu'avec d'autres éléments décoratifs.

Die zahlreichen farbenfrohen Möbel und Dekorationselemente gleichen die fehlenden Farben an Wänden und Säulen aus.

The columns and the furniture pieces placed around the area establish divisions that do not physically exist because the space is open and transparent.

Les colonnes et les pièces de mobilier installées autour de l'espace, instaurent un semblant de division virtuelle, sans nuire à la transparence et à l'ouverture qui le caractérisent.

Säulen und Möbel teilen den Raum auf, ohne dass eine physische Abtrennung existiert. Der Raum bleibt offen und transparent.

☐ Loop Telecom

Interior Designer: Roger Bellera

The aim of this project was to design the offices of a telecommunications company that specializes in corporate services in such a way that they would reflect the true image of the company. In order to emphasize the graphic and corporate image, it was decided to combine materials and colors while distributing spaces into clearly distinctive areas. The access to the lobby is located at one end of the rectangular floor and two areas framed by the outlines of intersecting ellipses divide the main space. By covering the floor with blue or green carpet—the colors of the company's logo—each area is defined visually as well as physically. The reception counter, set directly across from the entrance, was made of wood and aluminum complemented by corporate blue laminates. Display units have been placed at each end of the counter, and the access to the offices and work areas is located on the right, beyond the columns that are painted green to set off the entrance.

L'objectif de ce projet est la conception de bureaux d'une compagnie de télécommunications spécialisée dans des services sociaux, pour qu'ils reflètent l'image de marque de la compagnie. Accentuant le concept graphique de la société, les matériaux et les couleurs ont été combinés pour distribuer l'espace dans des zones distinctes. L'accès au lobby se situe à une extrémité du sol rectangulaire et deux zones encadrées par les contours de l'intersection de deux ellipses, divisent l'espace principal. Le sol recouvert d'un tapis bleu ou vert –les couleurs du logo de la compagnie– marque les contours visuels et physiques de chaque zone. Le comptoir de réception, installé en biais dans l'entrée, est en bois et aluminium, agrémenté de stratifié bleu. Les présentoirs sont placés aux extrémités du comptoir. L'accès aux bureaux est sur la droite, derrière les colonnes peintes en vert pour mettre en valeur l'entrée.

Ziel des Projektes war es, die Büroräume eines Telekommunikations- Unternehmens zu entwerfen. Dabei sollte das Corporate Image des Unternehmens in den Entwurf eingebunden werden. Es wurde entschieden, Material und Farben miteinander zu verbinden, die einzelnen Flächen aber in klar abgetrennte Bereiche aufzuteilen. Der Zugang zur Lobby befindet sich am Ende der rechteckig angelegten Etage mit zwei Bereichen, die von sich überschneidenden Elypsen eingerahmt werden, die den Hauptraum unterteilen. Dadurch, dass der Boden mit blauem oder grünem Teppich ausgelegt ist, bleibt jeder Bereich in sich geschlossen. Der Rezeptionstisch, der sich direkt gegenüber des Eingangs befindet, wurde aus Holz und Aluminium gestaltet, Laminate im Blau des Unternehmens setzen interessante Akzente. Zu beiden Seiten des Tresens sind Schauflächen angebracht und der Zugang zu den Büros und Arbeitsbereichen befindet sich rechts, direkt hinter den grünen Säulen.

The work areas are distributed in a large room in the interior of the building; they communicate with one another while also providing sufficient privacy.
Les zones de travail sont réparties dans une grande pièce à l'intérieur du bâtiment et communiquent entre elles, tout en bénéficiant d'une certaine intimité.
Die miteinander verbundenen Arbeitsbereiche befinden sich in einem langen Raum im Inneren und bieten die nötige Privatsphäre.

Glass panels on one side and a wooden module on the other divide the main space and define the different work areas.

Cloisons de verre d'un côté et module de bois, de l'autre, divisent l'espace principal et définissent les différentes zones de travail.

Glaswände auf der einen und Holzmodule auf der andere Seite teilen den Raum in verschiedene Arbeitsbereiche ein.

The furniture was custom-made to fit perfectly in the space and adapt to the company's requirements.

Le mobilier a été fait sur mesure pour intégrer parfaitement l'espace en harmonie avec les critères de la société.

Die maßgefertigten Möbel passen perfekt zu dem zur Verfügung stehenden Raum und den Anforderungen des Unternehmen.

☐ T. Stutzer Eggimann & Partner

Hemmi-Fayet Architects

The Hemmi-Fayet studio tackled the architectural challenge of endowing these offices for a Swiss legal firm with an image of reliability and order, while guaranteeing a modern and welcoming atmosphere. A restrained use of color and a narrow range of materials were the keys to fulfilling this objective. The design was developed on different levels, and the layout distributed the company's various functions according to the activities that are undertaken. Each space flows naturally and without any interference, creating orderly surroundings in which everything has its place and work can be carried out efficiently. The interior was painted completely white to make the fullest possible use of the light and make the space appear larger. This absence of color on the walls, floors, and ceiling provides a stark contrast with some of the dark furnishings and compositional elements. The appropriate lighting, efficiency of the decorative scheme and flexible furnishings create a bold, contemporary look.

Le studio Hemmi-Fayet a lancé le défi architectural de donner aux bureaux d'une société juridique suisse, une image reflétant la confiance et l'ordre, dans une atmosphère moderne et accueillante. L'emploi restreint de la couleur et l'éventail réduit de matériaux sont les éléments clés qui ont permis d'atteindre cet objectif. La conception prévoit plusieurs niveaux et le plan s'articule autour de la distribution des diverses fonctions de la compagnie selon les activités entreprises. Chaque espace, décloisonné, est marqué du sceau de la fluidité, créant un environnement ordonné où chaque chose a sa place et où le travail est efficace. L'intérieur est peint en blanc pour maximaliser l'effet de la lumière et agrandir l'espace. L'absence de couleur sur les murs, les sols et les plafonds tranche fortement avec certains meubles sombres et d'autres éléments décoratifs. L'éclairage idéal, la parfaite mise en scène du décor et les meubles modulables créent une atmosphère sobre et contemporaine.

Das Studio Hemmi-Fayet hat sich der Aufgabe gestellt, die Büroräume für ein schweizerisches Anwaltsbüro zu gestalten und dabei ein Image von Verlässlichkeit und Ordnung zu vermitteln, gleichzeitig aber modern und gemütlich zu wirken. Erreicht wurde dies durch den begrenzten Einsatz von Farbe und Material. Die einzelnen Funktionen des Unternehmens wurden auf unterschiedliche Ebenen verteilt. Jeder Bereich geht natürlich und übergangslos in den nächsten über und schafft eine geordnete Umgebung, wo alles an seinem Platz steht und die Arbeit effektiv ausgeführt werden kann. Die Innenräume wurden ganz in Weiß gehalten, um das Licht so weit als möglich auszunutzen und den Raum größer wirken zu lassen. Das Fehlen von Farbe an den Wänden, Böden und den Decken bietet einen starken Kontrast zu den dunklen Möbeln und Elementen. Eine angemessene Beleuchtung, Effizienz bei der Dekoration und flexible Möbel sorgen für einen modernen, klar strukturierten Eindruck.

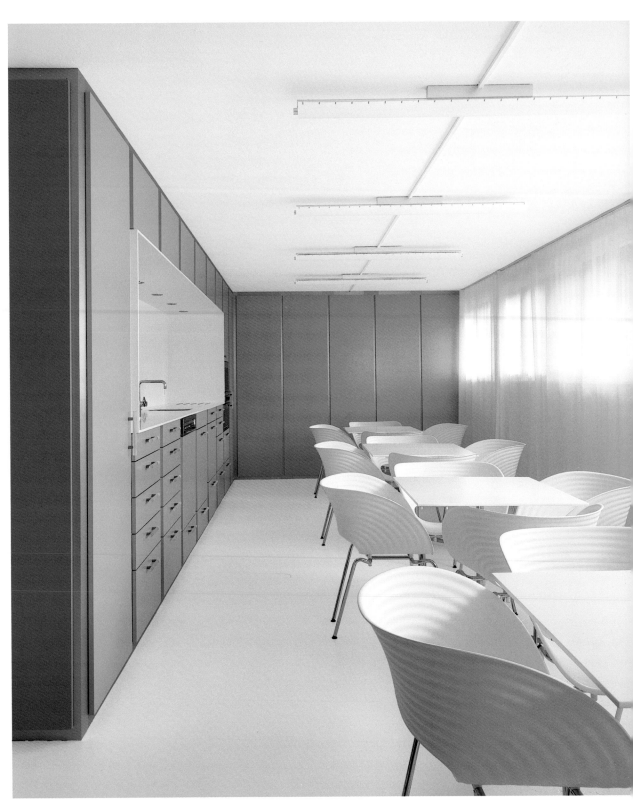

The interior was painted completely white to maximize the light and make the space appear larger. This absence of color in the walls, floors, and ceiling provides a stark contrast to the blue wall unit.

L'intérieur est entièrement peint en blanc pour maximiser l'impact de la lumière et agrandir l'espace. L'absence de couleur sur les murs, les sols et les plafonds contraste fortement avec le bleu de l'unité.

Das Innere ist komplett weiß und lässt den Raum heller und größer wirken. Das Weglassen von Farbe an Wänden, Böden und Decken erzeugteinen stacken kontrast zu der blauen Schrankwand.

The choice of wood for the flooring and the controlled palette of materials and colors contributes to the main objectives of the project - balance and pragmatism.

Le choix du bois pour les sols et la palette bien définie de matériaux et de couleurs répondent aux critères essentiels du projet - équilibre et pragmatisme.

Das Holz des Bodens und die beschränkte Palette an verwendeten Materialien und Farben stehen für Ausgewogenheit und Pragmatismus.

With the exception of two doors flanking either side of the hallway, the wall is made of glass; this serves to link the areas, enlarge the space, and take advantage of the natural light.

À l'exception de deux portes encadrant les deux côtés du hall d'entrée, le reste du mur est en verre pour unir les zones entre elles, élargir l'espace et tirer parti de la lumière naturelle.

Die von zwei Türen durchbrochene Glasmand nutzt das Tageslicht, verbindet die einzelnen Bereiche und lässt den Raum größer wirken.

☐ Osho International

Daniel Rowen

These offices, located on the 46th floor of the former GE tower on Lexington Avenue in New York City, serve as the headquarters of an international publishing company that specializes in subjects related to Zen and meditation. The aim was to create an office environment that reflects the spirit of the individuals who work in the company and the special characteristics of the material they deal with. The office design revolves around the consolidation of the elevator lobby, reception, and conference room as a single, large space. This central, communal area is defined by storage cabinets covering the walls on two sides, and by a floor-to-ceiling, translucent glass wall on the side facing the elevators. When seen from the entrance, this wall reflects the movement insides the various spaces and the shadows of the occupants. On the side by the hallway, the glass is deprived of its inherent transparency to provide privacy for the individual offices.

Ces bureaux, situés au 46e étage de l'ancienne tour GE sur la Lexington Avenue, à New York City, sont le siège social d'une compagnie d'édition internationale, spécialisée dans les thèmes relatifs au Zen et à la méditation. Le but était de créer un espace bureau reflétant l'esprit des individus travaillant dans la compagnie et les caractéristiques du sujet qu'ils traitent. Le design du bureau est axé sur la réunion en un seul grand espace de la zone ascenseur, de la réception et de la salle de conférence. Cette zone centrale commune se définit par des espaces de rangement plaqués sur les murs latéraux et par un mur de verre translucide, tout en hauteur, en face des ascenseurs. Dés l'entrée, le mur reflète les mouvements à l'intérieur des différents espaces et les ombres des occupants. Sur la face latérale de l'entrée, le verre perd de sa transparence pour préserver l'intimité des bureaux individuels.

Diese Büroräume, die im 46. Stockwerk des ehemaligen GE-Turms auf der Lexington Avenue in New York City untergebracht wurden, dienen als Hauptgeschäftsstelle einer internationalen Verlagsgesellschaft, die sich mit Themen wie Zen und Meditation befasst. Es sollte ein Umfeld geschaffen werden, das die Seele der einzelnen Mitarbeiter des Unternehmens widerspiegelt, aber auch die besondere Charakteristik der hier verlegten Bücher. Der Grundriss des Büros konsolidiert sich besonders um die Lobby mit den Fahrstühlen, dem Empfang und dem Konferenzraum, die alle drei in einem einzigen großen Raum untergebracht wurden. Dieser zentrale Gemeinschaftsbereich wird von Lagerschränken bestimmt, die auf beiden Seiten die Wände bedecken, sowie durch eine durchgehende Glaswand auf der gegenüberliegenden Seite der Fahrstühle. Dahinter erkennt man schemenhaft die Bewegungen der Mitarbeiter. Auf der Seite der Eingangshalle wurde das Glas abgedeckt, um den einzelnen Büroräumen eine gewisse Privatsphäre zu schenken.

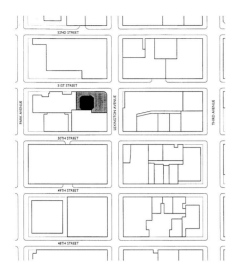

Plan Plan Grundriss

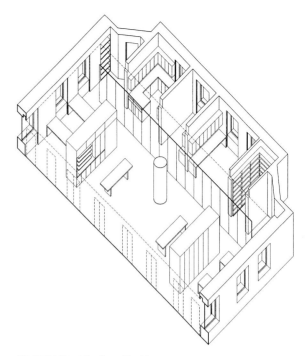

Perspective Perspective Perspektivzeichnung

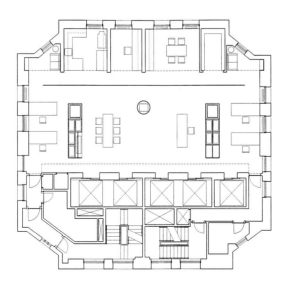

Ground floor Rez-de-chaussée Erdgeschoss

The translucent glass partition wall provides privacy from one side while reflecting the movement and shadows from passersby on the other side.

La cloison de verre translucide permet de garder un côté plus intime tout en reflétant le mouvement et les ombres des passants, de l'autre.

Die durchscheinende Glaswand schafft die nötige Privatsphäre und lässt gleichzeitig Bewegungen auf der anderen Seite erkennen.

☐ English Sport Council

Simon Conder Associates

The brief for this project was to remodel the reception area of the Sports Council, giving this government organization a professional image while making the entrance a friendly space that would make both visitors and employees feel welcome. The area is divided into two parts, one semi-private and the other public, separated by a wall enclosing the electrical installations and service facilities. The façade overlooking the street is made of glass in order to leave what is happening inside the building open to view from outside. The new exhibition gallery, with its stainless-steel structure and a large video screen on one of the vertical partitions, presents displays on photography, art and architecture and is clearly visible from the street. Simon Conder Associates took responsibility for the entire construction process, right down to the design of the furniture and the exhibition facilities. Here, small equals practical and the limited space allowed the team to effectively convey the building's role.

Le projet est de remodeler la zone de réception du Sports Council, dotant cette organisation gouvernementale d'une image professionnelle tout en transformant cette entrée en un espace agréable et accueillant pour les visiteurs et les employés. La zone est divisée en deux parties, l'une semi-privée et l'autre publique, séparées par un mur intégrant les installations électriques et les services. La façade donnant sur la rue est en verre, créant ainsi une transparence visuelle entre l'extérieur et l'intérieur du bâtiment. La nouvelle galerie d'exposition, une structure d'acier dotée d'un large écran vidéo sur une des cloisons verticales, expose des photos d'art et d'architecture. Elle est parfaitement visible depuis la rue. Le bureau Simon Conder Associates s'est chargé du processus de construction dans sa totalité, jusqu'au design des meubles et des éléments de la salle d'expositions. Ici, petit est synonyme de pratique et l'espace réduit permet à l'équipe de transmettre parfaitement la mission de l'édifice.

Ziel dieses Projektes war, den Empfangsbereich des Sportrates neu zu gestalten, und so dieser öffentlichen Behörde ein professionelles Image zu verleihen, deren Empfangsbereich alle Besucher willkommen heißt. Der Raum wurde in einen halbprivaten und einen öffentlichen Bereich unterteilt, die durch eine Wand voneinander getrennt sind, in der gleichzeitig die Verkabelung untergebracht ist. Die Fassade zur Straße wurde mit Glas verkleidet. Die neuen Ausstellungsräume, mit einer Struktur aus Edelstahl und einer großen Videoleinwand an einer der vertikalen Trennwände, zeigen Fotographien, Kunst und Architektur und sind von der Straße aus gut einzusehen. Simon Conder Associates hat den gesamten Bauvorgang beaufsichtigt, vom Design der einzelnen Möbel und Ausstellungseinrichtung bis hin zu den Ausstellungsräumen Gesamteindruck. "Klein" ist hier gleichbedeutend mit praktisch, denn der begrenzte Raum ermöglicht dem Team, der Rolle des Gebäudes effektiv zu entsprechen.

The reception and its surrounding area were designed to reflect the building's purpose as a practical information center.

La réception et la zone qui l'entoure ont été dessinées pour refléter la fonction du bâtiment : un centre d'information pratique.

Empfang und Eingangsbereich wurden entworfen, um den Zweck des Gebäudes als praktisches Informationscenter zu reflektieren.

Elevation Élévation Aufriss

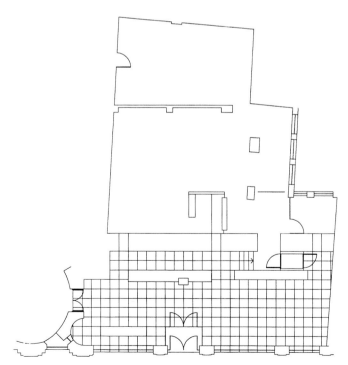

Plan Plan Grundriss

☐ Octagon

Francesc Rifé

These offices, located in a nineteenth-century building, were converted by the interior designer Francesc Rifé into a modern, avant-garde space that conserves the architectural essence of the past while also renovating the interiors in order to adapt them to the needs of the present and to the activities allocated to them. The construction consists of two nave-like structures joined by a central body set between them, with a total surface area of 1,600 sq. feet. The central area contains a staircase that provides a vertical link between the two spaces. The original ceilings and floors were left untouched wherever possible. The bright red that dots some of the walls, ceilings and separation panels sets up a contrast with the purity and coldness of the white, the metal structures, parquet floors, simple furniture and the elements left over from the building's past.

Ces bureaux, installés dans un bâtiment du XIXe siècle, ont été transformés par le designer d'intérieur Francesc Rifé en un espace avant-gardiste. L'architecte a su conserver l'essence architecturale du passé tout en rénovant les intérieurs pour les adapter aux besoins actuels et aux activités qu'ils abritent. La construction présente deux structures, à l'instar de nefs jointes par un corps central au milieu, sur une surface totale de 150 m². La zone centrale comprend un escalier, trait d'union vertical entre les deux espaces. Dans la mesure du possible, les plafonds et les sols d'origine sont conservés. Les larges touches de rouge qui ponctuent certains murs, plafonds et cloisons tranchent avec la pureté et la froideur du blanc, des structures de métal, des parquets, de la simplicité du mobilier et de certains éléments, réminiscences du passé industriel.

Diese Büros, die in einem Gebäude aus dem 19. Jh. liegen, wurden vom Innenarchitekten Francesc Rifé in einen modernen, avantgardistischen Raum verwandelt, der die architektonische Essenz der Vergangenheit bewahrt, und zugleich den Anforderungen der Gegenwart und den entsprechenden Aktivitäten entspricht. Der Bau besteht aus zwei, Langhaus ähnlichen Strukturen, die durch ein zentrales Element miteinander verbunden werden und so eine Gesamtfläche von 150 m² bieten. Im Zentralbereich gibt es ein Treppenhaus, das eine vertikale Verbindung zwischen den beiden Räumen herstellt. Die Originaldecken und -böden blieben so weit als möglich unangetastet. Leuchtend rote Akzente auf den Wänden, Decken und Trennwänden bieten einen Kontrast zum reinen und kühlen Eindruck der weißen Grundlage mit Metallstrukturen, Parkettböden, einfacher Möblierung und Elementen, die als Reminiszenzen an die Vergangenheit des Gebäudes mit in den Entwurf eingebunden wurden.

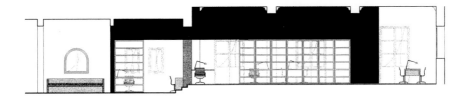

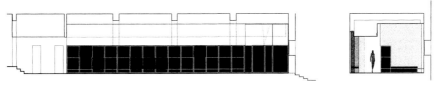

Elevations Élévations Aufrisse

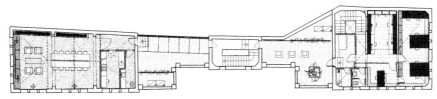

Second floor Deuxième étage Zweite Obergeschoss

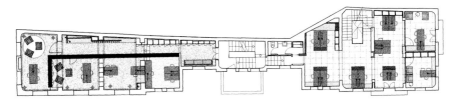

First floor Premier étage Erstes Obergeschoss

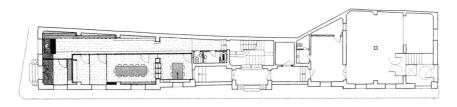

Ground floor Rez-de-chaussée Erdgeschoss

The construction consists of two nave-like structures joined by a central body with a staircase.

La construction repose sur deux structures en nef jointes par un volume central doté d'un escalier.

Der Bau besteht aus zwei hallenartigen Strukturen, die in der Mitte mit einer Zentraleinheit mit Treppe verbunden sind.

Although the old ceilings and floors were retained, striking, new elements have been integrated to provide an appealing contrast between past and present, and between new and old.
Tout en préservant les sols et plafonds d'origine, de nouveaux éléments originaux ont été ajoutés pour sublimer le contraste entre le passé et le présent, entre l'ancien et le moderne.
Die alten Decken und Böden wurden erhalten, es kamen jedoch neue Elemente hinzu, so dass ein attraktiver Kontrast entstand.

The intensity of the red dotting some of the walls, ceilings and separation panels contrasts with the purity and coldness of the white and the simplicity of the furniture.

L'intensité du rouge ponctuant certains des murs, plafonds et cloisons, contraste avec la pureté et la froideur du blanc et la simplicité de l'ameublement.

Die intensiv roten Farbtupfer an Wänden, Böden und Trennpaneelen kontrastieren mit dem reinen, kalten Weiß und den simplen Möbel.

The architects approached the restoration with the idea of preserving the existing structure as much as possible and so they kept the ceilings and floors where appropriate.

Dans ce projet de rénovation, en gardant les sols et les plafonds appropriés, les architectes ont décidé de préserver le plus possible la structure préexistante.

Die Architekten haben bei der Renovierung auf die Bewahrung der alten Strukturen gesetzt und Böden und Decken wo möglich erhalten.

☐ Mindfield

Shubin + Donaldson Architects

The aim of the prestigious publicity agency, Ground Zero, was to build up a postproduction company reflecting the same futuristic and unique design as their original offices. With this intention, Ground Zero commissioned Shubin + Donaldson, the same company that had designed those offices. The new post-production areas were set up in a building adjacent to the Ground Zero headquarters. Both buildings are separated by an alley which is beautifully integrated into the architectural ensemble and they reflect the homogeneity of the two spaces, maintaining a conceptual consistency. The new work areas are designed as open plans which are continually intersected by walls made of anodized aluminum, wood, steel and acrylic panels. The interior decoration, with ergonomic, state-of-the-art furniture, displays an attractive visual interplay of sophisticated and futuristic references. A dynamic, modern space has been created on the basis of daring but effective combinations of textures and materials.

L'objectif de cette prestigieuse agence de publicité, Ground Zero, est de construire une société de postproduction dotée du même design unique et futuriste que leurs bureaux d'origine. A ce titre, Ground Zero a engagé Shubin + Donaldson, la compagnie qui les avaient initialement dessinés. Les nouveaux locaux de postproduction sont installés dans un édifice contigu au siège social de Ground Zero. Une allée, merveilleusement intégrée à l'ensemble sépare les deux bâtiments, reflets de l'homogénéité des deux espaces dans une unité conceptuelle. Les nouveaux bureaux sont conçus comme des espaces ouverts, scandés par des cloisons en aluminium anodisé, en bois, en acier ou en acrylique. La décoration intérieure, dotée de meubles ergonomiques au style tendance, offre un mélange intéressant de touches à la fois subtiles et futuristes. Il en résulte un espace moderne, dynamique issu de l'alliance de textures et de matériaux audacieux, du plus bel effet.

Ziel der bekannten Werbeagentur Ground Zero war es, ein Postproduction-Unternehmen aufzubauen, in dem sich das futuristische und einzigartige Design des Originalbüros widerspiegelt. Shubin & Donaldson wurde mit dieser Aufgabe betraut, dasselbe Unternehmen, das auch schon die ersten Büroräume entworfen hatte. Die neuen Postproduction-Bereiche wurden in einem Gebäude direkt neben der eigentlichen Hauptgeschäftsstelle eingerichtet. Beide Gebäude sind durch eine Allee voneinander getrennt und wirken dennoch homogen. Die neuen Arbeitsbereiche sind offene Flächen, die kontinuierlich durch Wände aus eloxiertem Aluminium, Holz, Stahl und Acrylpaneelen unterbrochen werden. Die Innenausstattung mit ergonomischen, hochmodernen Möbeln bietet einen attraktiven Eindruck gut durchdachter, futuristischer Referenzen. So wurde ein dynamischer, moderner Raum auf der Basis einer gewagten, aber effektiven Kombination von Texturen und Material geschaffen.

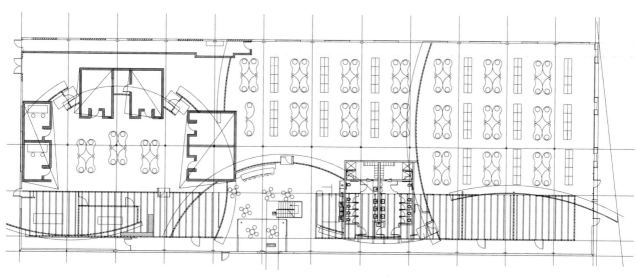

Plan Plan Grundriss

The reception is furnished with a semicircular metal table and a glass notice board with lighting incorporated. The coldness of these elements contrasts with the wooden beams and columns.

La réception possède une table de métal en hémicycle et un panneau d'affichage en verre avec éclairage intégré. La froideur de ces éléments contraste avec les poutres et les colonnes de bois.

Der Metalltisch und das beleuchtete Nachrichtenbrett aus Glas des Empfangs kontrastieren mit den Balken und Säulen aus Holz.

The interior decoration, with its ergonomic, state-of-the-art furniture, creates an attractive visual interplay of sophistication and futuristic echoes.

La décoration intérieure, dotée de son ameublement ergonomique et tendance, crée un magnifique jeu visuel de touches à la fois raffinées et futuristes.

Die Inneneinrichtung mit ergonomischen, ultra-modernen Möbeln gibt dem Raum eine elegante und leicht futuristische Note.

The striking volumes in the entrance provide a striking contrast with the design found inside, where the combinations of materials and textures establishes a distinctive, futuristic look.

Les volumes impressionnants de l'entrée créent un contraste surprenant avec le design intérieur où les mélanges de matériaux et de textures ont des allures originales et futuristes.

Das Design am Eingang kontrastiert deutlich mit dem im Inneren, das durch Materialien und Muster leicht futuristisch wirkt.

Ergonomic and functional furniture was chosen for the editing suites. The materials and colors are warmer and more comfortable than those in the other rooms.

Mobilier ergonomique et fonctionnel pour les pièces réservées à l'édition. Les matières et les couleurs sont plus chaudes et plus confortables que dans les autres pièces.

Für die Editionsbüros wurden ergonomische, funktionelle Möbel gewählt. Materialien und Farben sind wärmer als in den anderen Räumen.

☐ Unit-F

Rataplan

This architectural intervention, on pre-existing premises, sought to achieve a new flexible, multifunctional space designed to house the headquarters of a company in the fashion textile industry. The project consists of two levels arranged along the lines of a regular layout that provides an efficient distribution of space. The textile theme takes on great prominence in the design, and not only as a symbolic representation of the activity of the company. Textiles are important both esthetically and functionally, as they are used to shield the interiors from exterior light and allow it to be filtered at will. The use of mobile panels and sliding doors provides a means of marking out spaces, as well as greater freedom of movement between the different settings. This modern space is characterized by its ergonomic furniture, cold and metallic color scheme, and futuristic atmosphere, a marriage of usability and design.

Cette prestation architecturale sur des locaux préexistants, a tenté de réaliser un nouvel espace flexible et polyvalent, pour héberger le siège social d'une entreprise de l'industrie textile de mode. Le projet s'articule autour de deux niveaux agencés le long des lignes d'un plan régulier, offrant une distribution efficace de l'espace. Le design met en valeur le thème du textile sans en être uniquement la représentation symbolique. Les qualités esthétiques et fonctionnelles des textiles sont également mises en relief : ils protègent l'intérieur de la lumière extérieure qu'ils tamisent à volonté. Les cloisons mobiles et les portes coulissantes servent à délimiter l'espace et confèrent une liberté de mouvement dans les différentes zones. Cet espace moderne se définit par son mobilier ergonomique. Une mise en scène froide aux couleurs métalliques dans une ambiance futuriste parachève l'union entre l'utilitaire et le design.

Dieser architektonische Eingriff in bereits bestehende Räume sollte für einen neuen, flexiblen Bereich sorgen, in dem die Hauptgeschäftsräume eines Unternehmens aus der Modebranche untergebracht wurden. Das Projekt besteht aus zwei Ebenen, die auf der Basis eines regelmäßigen Grundrisses arrangiert wurden und so eine effiziente Verteilung des Raumes ermöglichen. Das textile Thema spiegelt sich im Design immer wider und nicht nur als symbolische Repräsentation der Aktivitäten dieses Unternehmens. Textilien sind sowohl ästhetisch als auch funktionell wichtig, da sie die Innenräume vom Außenlicht abschirmen und eine individuelle Filterung ermöglichen. Der Einsatz mobiler Trennwände und Schiebetüren bietet die Möglichkeit, Räume frei zu gestalten. Dieser moderne Raum wird von seiner ergonomischen Ausstattung, den kalten und metallischen Farbschemata und der futuristischen Atmosphäre bestimmt, eine enge Verbindung zwischen Nutzen und Design.

This modern space is characterized by ergonomic furniture and a range of cold, metallic colors that create a futuristic atmosphere.

Cet espace moderne se définit par un mobilier ergonomique et une palette de couleurs métalliques et froides, créant une ambiance futuriste.

Dieser moderne Raum ist durch ergonomische Möbel charakterisiert. Kühle Metallfarben schaffen eine futuristische Atmosphäre.

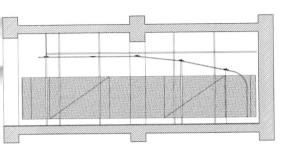

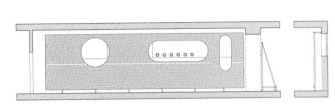

Sections Sections Schnitte

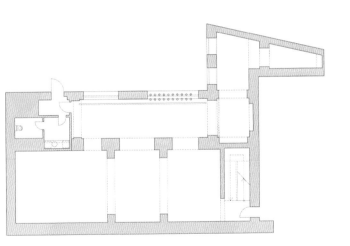

Ground floor Rez-de-chaussée Erdgeschoss

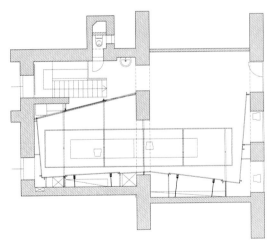

Second floor Deuxième étage Zweite Obergeschoss

165

The various rooms are spatially organized through the use of separating panels, sliding doors, or the placement of fabrics in some areas.

L'organisation spatiale de nombreuses pièces se fait grâce à des cloisons, des portes coulissantes et l'emploi de tissus dans certaines zones.

Die einzelnen Räume sind durch Trennwände, Schiebetüren und in einigen Bereichen durch Textilien voneinander getrennt.

☐ Raika Bank

Atelier Architect Andreas Schmitzer

The design of the Raika Bank in Salzburg represented an attempt to change the bank's classical image from an institution devoted exclusively to safeguarding money and securities into a place where information and transparency are essential values. The corporate image is conveyed by materials, shapes and colors that convey a sense of functionality and high technology. Some of the more private workspaces, such as the conference rooms, are separated from the main area by translucent floating panels. The circular shape of the workstations emphasizes the notion of mobile furnishings that can be moved around within the space. Three false ceilings hang in the foyer, providing warm, ambient lighting in orange tones throughout. A curved wall integrating and separating all the technical equipment creates a dynamic effect along the corridor. The play of warm and cold colors reinforces the formal characteristics of the project.

Le design de la banque Raika, à Salzbourg, tente de changer l'image de marque classique de la banque en tant qu'institution consacrée exclusivement à la sauvegarde de l'argent et des fonds, en un lieu dont les critères essentiels sont la transparence et l'information. L'image de la société se reflète dans les matériaux, les formes et les couleurs imprimés du sceau du fonctionnel et de la technologie de pointe. Des cloisons translucides et flottantes séparent, de la surface principale, certains des espaces plus privés, comme les salles de conférence. La forme circulaire des bureaux souligne la notion de meubles modulables au gré de l'espace. Trois faux plafonds suspendus au-dessus du foyer, dispensent partout une lumière ambiante chaleureuse dans les tons orangés. Un mur incurvé intègre et sépare la totalité de l'équipement technique, créant une ambiance dynamique le long du couloir. Le jeu de lumières froides et chaudes souligne les critères formels du projet.

Das Design der Raika Bank in Salzburg steht für den Versuch, das klassische Image einer Institution, die sich exklusiv der Aufbewahrung von Geld und Sicherheiten widmet, dahingehend zu ändern, dass hier ein Raum vorherrscht, in dem Information und Transparenz zu den herausragenden Werten gehören. Das Corporate Image wurde durch die Materialien, Formen und Farben unterstützt, die ein Gefühl von Funktionalität und High-Tech vermitteln. Einige der eher privaten Arbeitsplätze, wie z.B. die Konferenzräume, werden vom Hauptbereich durch transparente, hängende Trennwände abgeteilt. Die runden Arbeitsplätze verstärken den Eindruck mobiler Ausstattung und können innerhalb des Raumes umgestellt werden. Drei abgehängte Decken im Foyer sorgen für eine warme Beleuchtung in orangefarbenen Tönen. Eine gebogene Wand bietet einen dramatischen Effekt im Flur. Das Spiel mit warmen und kalten Farben unterstützt die formellen Charakteristiken des Projektes.

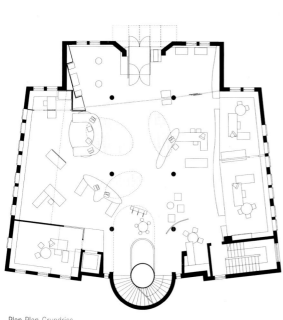

Plan Plan Grundriss

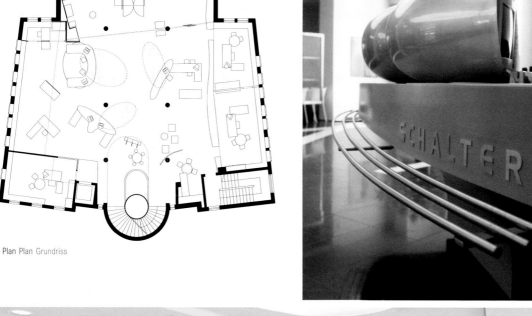

The curved wall that separates the technical and service area from the rest of the space creates a dynamic effect along the corridor.

Le mur incurvé qui sépare la zone de services et technique du reste de l'espace marque le long couloir de dynamisme.

Die gewundene Mauer trennt Service- und Technikbereich vom Rest und erzeugt entlang des Flurs einen dynamischen Effekt.

☐ Dalton's Digital Brothers

Mariano Martín Domínguez

The aim of the architect Mariano Martín was to create a project where functionality and esthetic impact go hand in hand. The client, a producer of commercials, required different rooms for different the phases of making and editing videos, each with its own acoustics, temperature control, and light requirements. Furthermore, the layout also had to incorporate a reception, administration zone, post-production room, and a kitchen-dining room that doubles as a loading and unloading area. The architectural solution resembled a well-organized white box, which could comfortably house both the service and the work areas. The interior could be described as a large gray volume made of polished cement, with vertical parameters and unadorned, reinforced concrete pillars fully exposed to view. The two administrative areas were enclosed in glass thus providing a source of natural light to the access hallway.

L'architecte Mariano Martín désirait créer un projet alliant l'impact esthétique et fonctionnel. Le client, producteurs de réclames publicitaires, voulait différentes pièces pour les différentes phases de fabrication et d'édition de vidéos, avec acoustique, contrôle de température et éclairage individuels. En outre, il fallait y incorporer une zone de réception, d'administration, une pièce pour la post-production et une salle à manger/cuisine faisant aussi office de zone de chargement et déchargement. La solution architecturale a opté pour une boîte blanche bien conçue, pouvant facilement héberger les services et les bureaux. L'intérieur est un vaste volume gris en béton poli, doté de plans verticaux et de simples colonnes en béton armé, très visibles. Les deux zones administratives sont entourées de verre, source de lumière naturelle pour le hall d'accès.

Der Architekt Mariano Martin wollte bei diesem Projekt Funktion und Ästhetik miteinander verbinden. Der Kunde, ein Werbefilmproduzent, bat um verschiedene Zimmer für die einzelnen Phasen der Videofilmherstellung, die jeweils über eigene Akustik-, Temperatur- und Beleuchtungssteuerungen verfügen müssen. Im Layout sollten darüber hinaus auch eine Rezeption, ein Verwaltungsbereich, ein Nacharbeitungszimmer und ein Küchen-/Essbereich, der auch als Lade- und Verladebereich dienen könnte, Platz finden. Der Innenbereich ist ein großer, grauer Raum aus poliertem Zement, der über senkrechte, ungeschmückte Parameter verfügt, die von frei stehenden Betonpfeilern getragen werden. Die beiden Verwaltungsbereiche wurden mit Glas verkleidet und sorgen so dafür, dass in den Eingangsflur natürliches Tageslicht einfällt.

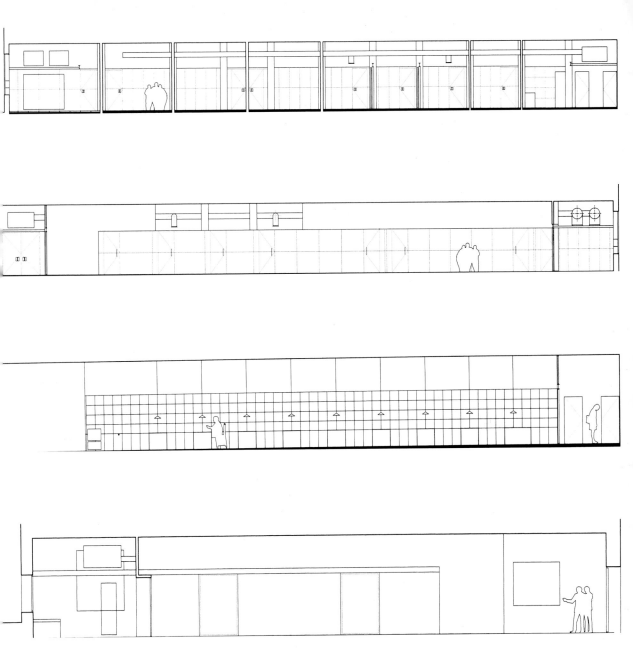

Longitudinal sections Sections longitudinales Längsschnitte

Iron and glass furniture was chosen for the rooms along the first axis. For those situated along the second axis, the iron was maintained but it was combined with beech wood.

Le mobilier, alliant le verre et le fer, décore les pièces le long du premier axe. Il conjugue le bois de bouleau et le fer, le long du second axe.

Möbel aus Eisen und Glas wurden für die Zimmer an der ersten Achse gewählt. Für die zweite Achse wurde Eisen mit Buche kombiniert.

Each room has its own acoustics, temperature control, and light (both natural and artificial) requirements, and these factors determined the course of the refurbishment from the outset.

L'acoustique, le réglage de température et de l'éclairage (naturel et artificielle) sont propres à chaque pièce. Ces critères de restauration ont été posés dès la conception.

Akustik, Klimatisierung und Beleuchtung sind für jeden Raum individuell geregelt und bestimmen die jeweilige Einrichtung.

A multi-use space designed as a rest area was provided. It can be used as a kitchen, dining room, and a loading and unloading area.

Un espace polyvalent conçu comme une zone de repos. Il peut faire office de cuisine, salle à manger et zone de chargement et déchargement.

Der als Pausenraum vorgesehene Mehrzweckraum kann als Küche, Esszimmer und Lade- und Entladezone genutzt werden.

Cross sections Sections transversales Querschnitte   Plan Plan Grundriss

☐ Office 21

Hank Mohen/ Milda International

The Office 21 occupies the 21st floor of a building in the center of the downtown area in Shanghai, overlooking the city's skyline. One of the main design premises was to guarantee the spatial fluidity of the space and take full advantage of the limited surface area. The company's creative character inspired the architects to come up with a dynamic, open space that also provides intimate areas where projects could be developed in privacy. The careful arrangement of materials like the glass partitions defines that spatial quality and accentuates the mythical references of the architectural concept. A public conference room is located in the center of the space and marks a nexus between the other rooms, maintaining the dynamic flow. Light and shadow play an important role and every object receives natural or artificial light, which is deflected or absorbed according to its texture, thereby transforming these objects into distinctive sculptures.

Office 21 occupe le 21e étage d'un bâtiment situé au cœur de Shanghai et surplombe la ligne d'horizon de la cité. L'une des priorités majeures du design était de garantir la fluidité spatiale et de tirer parti au maximum de l'espace restreint. Influencés par l'élan novateur de cette compagnie, les architectes ont créé un espace ouvert et dynamique doté aussi de zones privées plus intimes, propices à l'étude et à la création de projets. L'agencement parfaitement pensé des matériaux définit la qualité de l'espace, à l'instar des cloisons de verre, qui exaltent les schémas mythiques du concept architectural. Une salle de conférence publique occupe le centre de l'espace et son emplacement crée un lien entre les autres pièces, tout en maintenant la fluidité dynamique de l'espace. L'ombre et la lumière y jouent un rôle important et chaque objet reçoit la lumière naturelle ou directe, renvoyée ou absorbée selon sa consistance, métamorphosant ainsi les objets en sculptures uniques.

Office 21 befindet sich auf der 21. Etage eines Gebäudes in der Innenstadt von Shanghai. Vor hier aus hat man einen herrlichen Blick auf die Skyline der Stadt. Eine der wichtigsten Vorgaben an die Designer war, die begrenzte Fläche so gut wie möglich zu nutzen. Es wurde ein dynamischer, offener Raum geschaffen, der aber auch Räume enthält, in denen einzelne Projekte in Ruhe bearbeitet werden können. Die sorgfältige Auswahl des Materials bestimmt diese Räumlichkeit, so zum Beispiel die Glastrennwände, welche die mythischen Muster des architektonischen Konzeptes unterstreichen. In der Mitte befindet sich ein Konferenzraum, dessen Position die Verbindung zu den anderen Zimmern markiert und so den Eindruck von Dynamik vermittelt. Licht und Schatten spielen eine große Rolle und jedes Objekt wird von natürlichem oder künstlichem Licht beschienen, was die verschiedenen Objekte in einzigartige Skulpturen verwandelt.

Plan Plan Grundriss

The reception counter, set directly across from the entrance, was made of glass, complemented by a built-in lighting system.

Le comptoir de réception, qui traverse l'entrée, est en verre et dispose d'un éclairage intégré.

Der Rezeptionstisch, der sich direkt gegenüber des Eingangs befindet, wurde aus Glas gestalten und mit einem eingebauten Beleuchtungssystem ergänzt.

The Chinese characters, adorning the entrance door, create a bold, contemporary atmosphere

Les caractères chinois, au-dessus de la porte d'entrée, créent une atmosphère contemporaine ponctuée d'originalité.

Die chinesischen Schriftzeichen die die Eingangstür schmücken erzeugen eine kühne, zeitgenössische Atmosphäre.

The open space also provides more intimate areas where projects can be developed in privacy.

L'espace ouvert permet aussi d'avoir des zones plus intimes, propices au développement de projets à caractère plus privé.

Innerhalb des offenen Raumes gibt es auch Zonen, in denen einzelne Projekte in Ruhe bearbeitet werden.

Photo credits Crédits photographiques Fotonachweis